Vibrate

Heal Yourself Like No One Else Can

Gráinne McNamara

Published by **Elevation Publishing Group**

The information contained in this book is provided solely for educational and informational purposes.

Disclaimer

This book is intended for educational and informational purposes only. It is not intended to diagnose, treat, cure, or prevent any disease.

The content reflects the author's personal research, experiences, and interpretations of traditional and contemporary approaches to healing and self-inquiry. While every effort has been made to ensure accuracy, the author and publisher make no representations or warranties regarding the completeness or applicability of the information presented.

Herbal remedies, plant-based practices, and other wellness modalities may not be appropriate for everyone and may interact with medications or existing medical conditions. Readers are encouraged to consult a qualified healthcare professional before beginning any herbal regimen, dietary change, or wellness practice, particularly if pregnant, nursing, managing a medical condition, or taking prescription medications.

The author and publisher disclaim any liability for any adverse effects or outcomes resulting from the use or application of the information in this book.

References to specific traditions, practices, practitioners, or products are provided for informational purposes only and do not constitute endorsement.

Dedication

For Ciara, my firstborn, my teacher, my inspiration.

Though I was not always home, you showed me that an open heart cannot be broken.

You reminded me that home is where you feel safe to be yourself and to love.

May this book honor the courage, wisdom, and resilience you carry-and remind us both that the greatest teacher and healer lives within.

Table of Contents

CHAPTER 1

CONSTELLATIONS

In Ireland, the stars sing in the night sky. They form a picture, like notes on a page of sheet music. With no telescopes to inspect them, I would draw the patterns of the song they sang in my mind, stringing together a lyric of constellations. A starry song of my own design.

Each time I looked up to the expanding universe, I was filled with a sense of expansion within myself. Those stars shone in all the lands I hoped to one day explore. They were my one connection to a bigger world outside my little rural Irish town.

In my spirit, their song to me was that the universe would provide opportunities for me to expand—if only I worked hard and took the plunge into the unknown. Perhaps those stars would provide me the bridge to explore new cultures, to cross over to faraway lands more prosperous than my own, lands with prestigious work that would come to dominate my own experience of the world.

All my youth, I was obsessed with the skies. I'd spend hours watching them, day and night. In the day, I'd notice the impact the skies had upon the tides and wind—a wind intermingled with the whispers of faeries and saints. A sense of wonderment flowed through me, a sense that all was connected—mind, body, spirit, and Creation itself.

And yet mere miles from our town was the greatest symbol of disconnection—the border between Ireland and Northern Ireland. The contentious border cut through our island not only in a geopolitical sense, but spliced our identities into labels. Catholics and Protestants, pro-unification Republicans and pro-UK Unionists.

Born in the midst of the Troubles, the sectarian conflict raging mirrored the conflict within our home. Raised by parents born in near-poverty, it was economic insecurity that fueled my desire to leave Ireland, not a lack of love for the land itself.

For all the difficulties around me, there was also much beauty. I was surrounded by poets and philosophers capable of finding meaning in every stone and blade of grass. Their influence fed my curiosity, forming the foundation of continuous learning which has shaped my life since.

I would find myself scarred both physically and emotionally for years as the result of a tumultuous family life. A father who belittled and abused me and a mother who wondered with exasperation why I could not "be like the other girls." A message formed in my mind: My thoughts were too big for the life I had been born into. My dreams too unreachable. Like the stars above.

Under the weight of this message, I tried to end it all. At only thirteen years old.

Thankfully, my suicide attempt was *not* to be the end of my story. When I rose from the depths, a new message formed: I did not want to die. But I did want *out*. Escape. To redefine and recreate myself. To unshackle my identity from the circumstances of my birth. To expand my limits so I could reach the stars. I would fight. And I would win.

As an adult, the world of finance offered me an escape from poverty and the pain of feeling alone and misunderstood. Despite my corporate "handicaps," that is, being Irish and being a woman, I carved a path forward; first in the London banking world and eventually on Wall Street.

Over the years, I would start a family, go through divorce, and make a name for myself at the intersection of finance and technology, working my way to the heights of corporate America. I had become a star in one dimension, but the toll extracted on the other aspects of my own self battled for attention until they became impossible to ignore.

In an increasingly connected world, why did I still feel the pain of disconnection? Why did the various pieces of myself feel like they were galaxies apart? I had achieved what so many women hope to achieve—financial prosperity, motherhood, and even philanthropic involvement. Still, I felt a dark, gaping distance between the person I was—and the person I wanted to be.

I had not escaped. Not truly. I had only designed a shinier cage for myself.

Perhaps you can relate. Perhaps you have even labeled this cage "success." All the while knowing you are deceiving yourself. You want to be a star—but remember, even stars can flicker and burn out.

In February of 2023, I did what the twenty-five-year-old version of myself would consider unthinkable. I "fired myself" and walked away from a seven-figure salary, with no new job title, no new salary in place. Selling my time for money was something I could not abide. The idea of trading time for money rather than outcomes was no longer an available option for my life.

Also, I was disquieted by the idea of devoting my intellect to learn concepts like artificial intelligence while neglecting my own *intuitive* intelligence.

Instead, I was consumed by a call to lean into the lessons about what it means to be human in this world.

You might ask why I would walk away, and it's fair to ask. By all external measures, I was doing well for myself. If you considered each individual facet of my life from a distance, it shone like a star. But internally, I could only feel the darkness. A darkness I had been running from for three decades. I walked away from all I had achieved for one reason:

I had lost myself.

Now it was time to *face* the darkness if I was to ever find myself whole again.

Many working women I have met face a similar story of finding their sense of being, their mental health teetering on the brink. They are trying to "have it all" as our mothers had hoped for—the perfect job title, the perfect family, the perfect generosity. They swap out masks for each role they have to play as they navigate the modern world. All at once, they feel like they have twenty characters they have to play while losing their own identity, their own sense of "self." They want to shine like stars, but end up feeling pulled into a black hole of despair, addictions, and loss of purpose.

We all are in search of the Divine Feminine. An energy that represents peace, harmony, connection to self, others, and Mother Nature.

Yet the Divine Feminine is *not* about gender. Feminine energy is available to be accessed by all humanity. We all exhibit the qualities of both masculine and feminine energy—like *yin* and *yang*, they must coexist in balance. Yet in my case, I had delved so deep into masculine energy, I had lost the feminine vibrations.

Like light itself, energy exists on a spectrum. The higher vibrations of masculine energy exhibit qualities such as confidence, discipline and strong decision making. Women need these energies to thrive. The lower vibrations of masculine energy exhibit oppression and dominance. Men and women alike must avoid these.

Meanwhile, energy classified as feminine also has lower and higher vibrations. On the low end, it displays manipulation and jealousy. On the higher end, it displays love, creativity and connection. Men and women both need these higher levels of feminine energy.

The stars above us have auras—energy they give off in the form of light, radio waves, and gravitational pull. Likewise, we humans have auras—*chakras*—centers of energy within us. When aligned, they form a constellation of internal harmony. When misaligned, we feel out of control, chaotic, and in conflict with self and others.

Deep down, we are seeking balance between the Divine Feminine and the Divine Masculine. Yet the balance—the good vibes—elude us. Why?

Because to find the light, you must cross the darkness.

We must digest what we ingest. We must put our own pain down first. We do not merely tell stories—we *live* them. For narrative is *emergent,* not absolute.

In my own narrative, I had to stop the ride and get off. Somewhere along the way, I lost the plot. I had not fully ingested what had happened to me as a child. Instead, I had drowned out my own pain rather than healed. The story I told myself for thirty years was that I could not exist without a weapon or a shield in hand at all times.

A new narrative was needed. A truer narrative. One where I would come to realize I was not a victim of anything, nor the sacrifice of anyone. Although I had been witness to much injustice and pain, that did not have to define who I was.

Finally, after fifty-one years on this earth and thirty years in corporate halls, I came to see how the greatest gifts given to me had been there all along. The truth of the matter was I had allowed my own light to dim, and when your internal light dims, the darkness only grows.

With this realization, I made a commitment that I would no longer succumb to the darkness. As I embarked on my healing journey, my thoughts turned back to the skies:

What if none of us are meant to be stars?

What if we were meant to be constellations?

A TRINITY OF BEING

Not long after I left my job focused on Wall Street, I was swimming with literal sharks in the Galapagos Islands. It was freeing to be in nature in contrast to the boardrooms I had left behind in New York.

And yet even in those ancient waters, the force of change is ever-present. Our guide shared about his observations of El Niño, and the climate changes being caused by humanity.

He saw an acceleration of change—the speeding up of the natural cycles. And I thought to myself, "No wonder we all feel out of balance. Nature is sending us a message."

There along the equator, at the center of the earth, my eyes turned upwards again to the stars above, visible like I had never seen them before. Once more, they sang to me.

In fact, we know now that stars emit radio waves, meaning science has proved what I knew as a little girl—*the stars do sing*. I felt safe and I felt whole. Captivated by the stories of the resilience and adaptations of the species witnessed by Darwin and his contemporaries in this magical place.

If the stars sing, then constellations are the choir, the symphony. Constellations have long been singing to humanity, shaping our destinies. Indigenous farmers still use the constellations as a marker for when to sow and when to reap. They are Nature's calendar, displaying eternal wisdom in their brilliance.

Holy men have used the constellations to tell stories and pass on ancient wisdom that cuts to the core of the human condition—conflict, but also healing. Across cultures, you will find religion, folklore, and heritage enshrined in the sky. Ever since the beginning of human history, navigators have used the constellations to chart their way across dark seas, whether in the spirit of discovery or economy.

Constellations are *universal*. Each ancient people had their own collection of stars, yet some asterisms like Orion, the Big Dipper, or the Southern Cross have been recognized across many cultures before they ever interacted with each other. For instance, when Europeans arrived in North America, they discovered the indigenous Americans also recognized Ursa Major as a bear. Humanity's common ground is not on the ground at all— it is in the heavens.

And yet, constellations are a fabrication. They only exist because we form them in our imagination. They exist because we have willed them into existence with our own intuitive intelligence and imagination.

From a scientific standpoint, the stars within a constellation have no true relation to one another. They are millions of miles apart from one another, separated by the vast void of space. And yet we also know that everything within the universe is held together by the invisible force of gravity.

From our vantage point on Earth, the stars within constellations are mesmerizing pinpoints of light. Yet were you to travel to them, you would find blazing, tumultuous, kaleidoscopic self-sustaining engines of energy, too powerful to approach without being consumed in the blaze. Our own local star, the sun, is the source of life for our little planet—it is generative. No wonder so many of the ancients worshiped it.

In constellations, we find a trinity of elements—light (stars), darkness (space), and the invisible lines we "draw" to connect them (imagination). With these three elements, we create stories. The bull Taurus charging the warrior Orion. The African queen Cassiopeia forced to sacrifice her daughter Andromeda, who is then rescued by Perseus.

Each story is made of light and dark, conflict and conquest. So why should we expect our lives to be any different? The story only happens when we cross the darkness to connect the points of light.

Constellations are a trinity of philosophy, nature, and spirituality. We can also see them as a trinity of elements forming human nature—mind, body, and spirit. It is in the mind—the imaginary lines between the stars—where the real work must be done.

Without the mind drawing the invisible lines, there is no constellation. There is no wholeness. No story.

When it comes to mental health, women of the Western world are in crisis. We discuss mental health and self-care more than ever before, yet we still feel lost on what to *do*.

Technology allows us to be more connected through digital spaces, yet women are grappling with isolation and loneliness,even as they may be surrounded by coworkers, spouses, children, and neighbors. We feel alone, yet so many of us are struggling with the same fundamental issue at the core. We need to come home to ourselves.

If we are honest with ourselves, we are trying to be stars in every dimension that exists; in the workplace, in the home, in our communities. We are constantly shifting from one role to another, feeling disconnected and dissonant, trying to keep each box separate so we can maintain some sense of sanity.

To be a woman, first and foremost, is frequently unsafe and lonely when feelings of extreme vulnerability and exhaustion are the norm.

Yet this compartmentalization is what is destroying us. For we are not meant to be simply stars lighting up the night sky alone. We are meant to be constellations. We are meant to work in harmony with the light that exists within our fellow humans. To align our own internal energy with the needs of the communities where we build a sense of belonging and meaning in this life.

We must be wary of the danger of succumbing to the intellectual mind, of believing the answers lie there alone. The Renaissance philosopher and scientist Descarte once observed, "I think, therefore I am." Yet to amend his philosophy, we must say, "I am, therefore I think. I feel, therefore I am also human."

For it is in the collective experience of mind, body, and spirit that we shape our existence. Not through what we think alone, but through what we feel. Also, we must consider how others feel as a result of what we do and think. For like the stars, our gravitational forces impact one another.

To become constellations—in our beings and in community—we have to become aware of our vibrations, our "vibes." We must channel the powerful energy within us to elevate, to find the balance between the Feminine and Masculine Divine.

If we are to integrate the pieces of ourselves, we must channel the light within us to cross the chasm of darkness that obstructs our way.

Typically, this is a journey into our trauma, a quest to understand what needs healing so we can show up fully embodied as our authentic selves. We must wield our intuitive intelligence to bring the dissonant pieces of our being into resonant vibration.

Only then can we connect the bright stars of our nature. Only then can we break the shackles of loneliness and separation to constellate mind, body, and spirit.

The journey is difficult, though. It requires you to first lose yourself. Perhaps you are already there. The good news is you've already completed the first step.

From there, you will find yourself. This is the difficult work that many will never go through because it means confronting the trauma, being honest with yourself, and facing the demons. But the true you is waiting on the other side.

Finally, you find others. This fascinating journey is about so much more than knowing yourself. Once you have found yourself, you can find meaningful connections with others who share life's journey with us.

Lose yourself.

Find yourself.

Find others.

This is the trinity of our journey.

THE HEROINE'S JOURNEY

The healing journey I went on forced me to turn my eyes to the heavens—literally and figuratively. It taught me to reconnect with myself through various healing practices, especially yoga and deep meditation. It has taught me to find the stars of my nature, cross the darkness, and form the constellation of who I truly am at the core.

I know this can run the risk of being romanticized. Yet many parts of the journey were painful. Before you can find yourself, you have to admit you've lost yourself. For most, we lost ourselves in the traumas we've faced, the disappointments, the betrayals.

Therefore, to find myself it meant reconnecting with my past, reconnecting with my heritage, reconnecting with the pain I had been fleeing for years. It meant looking at the worst parts of myself—the wrongs done to me by others, the wrongs I've done to myself, and the wrongs I've done to others.

From attempting to take my own life, battling depression, and sometimes the sheer terror that someone would come to "expose me" and take it all away, I was riddled with deep existential fear that drove much of my behavior. For years, I covered this fear up through addiction and attachments to the material world—the outward trappings of wealth.

In 2023, when I quit my job, for the first time in my life, I fully accepted that the only way to feel whole again was to stare the demons down and to go inside to heal myself. The most amazing part of the journey I embarked on was the knowledge that I was not alone.

While I did not start life from a place of privilege, life has put me in a position of one now. Rather than waste that privilege on myself, I feel a heavy sense of duty—an urgency—to be a voice for those who have none. Life has brought me to a place where I can be an emissary. My discoveries were too profound, too impactful to keep to myself.

I recognize not everyone has the opportunity to walk away from a job as I did. Yet we all deserve to heal and to feel safe and whole. Which brings us to why I decided to write this book.

In my own story of healing, one of the great sources of hope came through the women I met along the way. Women whose stories were their own—and yet I could not help but notice symmetry and intersections with my own experience.

We had similar pains, similar struggles, and similar insights into healing. Though one constellation is different from another, they share traits, they share proximity, they share *stories*. So it was with these women.

The next chapter will focus on my own story—the traumas I've had to revisit and how I've come to reconcile them with who I am today. Then you will hear about how yoga is a portal for me into the wisdom of the body and my reclamation of my own sovereignty in healing. In the subsequent chapters, my story will intersect with the stories of the other women I met along the way—women of varying backgrounds on their own healing journeys. In both the intersections and divergences of our pain, we weave a collective story of hurt, hope, and healing.

You'll meet Tatiana, a Russian woman grappling with her heritage and a self-destructive drive for perfection. In her journey, she discovered how claiming your birthright is about reconciling the pain and beauty in your background.

Next, you'll meet Sherri, a working mother tainted by a toxic workplace and trying to rediscover her femininity. In her story, you'll see how she rediscovered and embraced the power of love.

And finally, you'll meet Tamara, an accomplished advertising professional who left her career behind to confront her alcoholism and suicidal depression and open a yoga studio. With her, you'll see the power of release to unleash your full potential.

Their collective tales of mental health and self-discovery synchronized with my own—and my hope is they synchronize with yours, too. Together, they paint a portrait of the common struggles faced by today's working woman. From these intersecting journeys, an epic story is formed—a *Heroine's* Journey in search of the Divine Feminine energy.

I met these women in the US, in India, and in South America—all of them searching for their true nature, just like me. From plant medicine and whole food diets, to yoga, meditation, and communing with nature, the experiences of what we found were remarkably similar—even when our backgrounds and methodologies differed.

All of these interventions, therapies, and collective experiences seemed to point to one universal truth—methods to your healing can be found within.

In each journey, you'll see a process of self-transformation I like to refer to as an alchemy of pain. That is, you'll see pain transformed into beauty. This is the journey of all the great stories throughout time. Rags to riches. Enslaved to the pearly gates. Welcome home. Your carriage awaits.

My hope is that in these stories, you will see yourself. You may not go on the same physical journey—but we can all go on the metaphysical journey together. May their stories help you identify the path to healing, whatever your circumstances. The lessons here are strong, yet flexible, like an expert yogi.

The process is not an exact recipe—for only you can be you. Your exact path to healing will not look like mine. As such, approach with a sense of cautious curiosity. You do not need to emulate every practice described.

Never betray who you know yourself to be at your core—your values and beliefs. But do not hesitate if you discover a practice here that helps you find the light, helps you cross the darkness to form the beautiful constellation you are meant to be.

Many methods work for different people to connect with their inner selves, and many people need medical help to recover from the trauma they have encountered. Equally, depending on culture or belief systems or proximity to guides and teachers, some of the methods described will not be accessible to all.

The stories of these healing methods and practices serve as a backdrop to the bigger story here—how so many of us are desperately seeking some way to heal from fear, loneliness, and separation. Yet sharing the stories is how we help others know they are not alone and that many paths are available to those who seek to know themselves more deeply and authentically.

Ultimately, the stories here are chapters of a larger, epic journey we find ourselves in—the search for the Divine Feminine we have lost along the way. In this search, love is at the center. It is the binding force between mind, body, and spirit. Love for yourself, love for nature, and love for others.

When we are able to put our own pain in context and heal ourselves, we can literally expand our own light energy. We elevate the vibration from within the field of consciousness and it impacts the collective experience. When the light in me sees the light in you, we form a collective constellation that illuminates a galaxy of unlimited potential, love, and sisterhood.

Many call this "unity consciousness," a level of vibration that goes beyond oneself and is capable of resonating with all living souls. It is through developing awareness of our own vibrations that we can start to understand the complex effect of other vibrations in our collective sphere.

I'm aware that much of the talk around "vibrations" can be taken as more philosophical or spiritual. However, there is a scientific basis to it as well.

The late Dr. David R. Hawkins was an esteemed psychiatrist and researcher who conducted research focused on scientifically quantifying human consciousness and emotions. To do so, he developed a scale where different emotional states were assigned numerical values (from 0 to 1000) based on the vibrational frequency of the emotional state.

In his research, he found that emotions such as shame, guilt, and apathy register lowest on the scale, whereas emotions like love, joy, and enlightenment registered higher. Perhaps this is the exhilarating "tingle" we feel in such moments.

But did you know there were emotions and states of consciousness that had even higher vibrational frequencies? Can you guess what they were?

Authenticity and integrity.

These two emotional states registered among the highest vibrations on the scale. Dr. Hawkins claimed that when individuals embody authenticity and integrity, they resonate at a higher frequency. This resonance has a positive effect on not only the individual's own well-being but also on the world around them.

Dr. Hawkins went on to call this "the Map of Consciousness®." He showed that a higher consciousness (vibration) radiated a beneficial and healing effect on the world, verified in the human muscle response, which stays strong in the presence of love and truth.

In contrast, non–true or negative energy fields, which "calibrate" below the level of integrity, induced a weak muscle response. His work detailed a path to "enlightenment" where compassion, kindness, humility, reverence, and surrender are part of the process to elevate the vibrational frequencies we emanate for the sake of healing oneself and the world.

Elevating the vibration is what happens when we channel the collective energies of mind, body, spirit, nature, and community. When we elevate our own vibration to the higher levels of energy, we can integrate our energies. When we integrate, we elevate. Vibration is the invisible force that crosses the darkness to connect the stars of our being.

No matter how bright they may shine, stars cannot tell stories on their own. Only *constellations* can do so.

To become constellations, we must integrate the triune elements of our being—mind, body, and spirit. We must shed the labels we use to mask our authentic selves. We must recognize the beauty in pain. To find the light, we must first face the darkness.

CHAPTER 2

COIS TINE

My people come from a land where it's cold and damp, rural and remote. We had to convene inside to escape the sting of the elements. Either in a family house or the public house, we would gather with others from the *clan*.

These gatherings were sacred spaces we created—where discussions of both spiritual and human nature came together in unison. Not the language of intellectual endeavors, but the *craic* as we called it—what you might call chit-chat, though that's a far too flippant translation. For us, the meaning is deeper, more profound, and more rooted in our shared heritage.

At the fireside within each others' homes, we warmed ourselves with hot tea, conversation, and the brimming of life itself. *Cois tine* means "fireside" in Irish—the place where we expose what we know in the context of connecting with others. In the *cois tine*, people and ideas integrate. We pray together, we play together, and we create a vision of a world moving toward progression. The circle of life as we see it in Ireland.

Ancient wisdom. Modern expressions. Human senses. All three would vibrate in the air, incensing. In the sharing of words, we can make a symphony from the noise. We don't come into the world with an instruction manual, yet if we have a tongue in our mouths, we should use it. To speak. To sing. To taste. To laugh. To live.

You won't find many towns more centrally located in Ireland than Tullamore. When we lived there, we often had *cois tine* at my Uncle Jimmy and Aunt Maisie's home. The elders, having weathered the most winters, sat near the fire.

Yet because this was also my favorite place, I would find an excuse to get closer to the flickers of light and feel the blaze on my cheek, the rich scent of burning peat moss and smoke filling the air, a Kimberley mikado biscuit (a cookie) in hand. Or if we were lucky, we would be delighted by Aunt Mary's baking—the open range oven breathing out the crisp smell of homemade apple tarts or scones.

The rest of the adults stood about, engaged in lively conversation, including my parents, their words mingled with the chicory coffee or tea that was way too 'boiled' in their mugs. Every so often, one of the adults would slip me a taste, not that I needed the caffeine.

If a spare lap could not be found at these gatherings, the children could be found littered on the floor—that is, until it came time for the talent show. After the formal conversation, we would entertain the adults with singing, dancing, reading a poem, or showing a sketch—a lively form of "show and tell" where everyone was celebrated.

In *cois tine*, the artistic and practical are married together. Many nights, the women would crochet beautiful artisanal doilies as they spoke. Everyone had knitted clothing produced from such nights—a sweater, a scarf, a jumper—and in that way, we wore the *cois tine* on our skin, carrying it with us.

Auntie Mary was not only a great baker, but an expert in knitting beautiful designs. Sometimes she sold these, taking *cois tine* to the marketplace where it became a part of the local economy. Yet watching her, selling her wares was not her primary motive. The energy she put into knitting was like her form of meditation—a mantra of sorts, like praying the Rosary with its comforting rhythmic pattern.

The rhythms came through in the dancing, too—*one, two, three—one, two, three—one, two, three, four, five, six, seven.* The basic steps we all learned were the Walls of Limerick and the Siege of Ennis, connecting history to art and movement. It was impossible not to touch one another, what with the number of people packed together.

Every home had certain mainstays—you would find the rosary beads, the Brigid's Cross, the Tara brooch, the Irish cross, Padre Pio and Pope John Paul. Alongside these, you could find a picture of John F. Kennedy, who we saw as the ideal for Irish potential. In today's world, this intertwining of religion and state feels foreign, but in 1970s Ireland, it was the norm. In all these symbols were woven together history, folklore, spirituality, and possibility. We were raised to be faithful to the heavens and patriotic to the tricolor with its green, white and gold as symbols of the earth, the sun and the air itself. Sacred, elemental and life-sustaining.

But *cois tine* was not only in the private homes—it could also be found in the public spaces. The local public house was where people would gather to talk about matters, including politics, since Ireland was in the midst of The Troubles and sectarian violence happening along the border. I like to think they solved many problems with bottles of porter beer and sidecars of Paddy Power whiskey—in a crystal glass, if you were lucky.

In the "snugs" of the public houses—quiet spaces—the conversations were sacred. No big screen televisions broadcasting football games to distract from the person beside you. All who were present knew the rules of engagement. "We don't bow down to anyone down here," was often quoted.

While it was often the men who would gather after work, families were not strangers to these spaces, especially on a Sunday. It was the place to grab a Sunday dinner after mass. Luxuries were rare, so we would get "Tayto" chips—the cheese and onion-flavored chips were my favorite. And while the adults might enjoy their libations, we children might get a Red Lemonade, which had no actual lemons in it but was like our version of Coca-Cola.

Between swigs, we could crunch on our chips or the dry-roasted peanuts or bacon fries—so long as we did not interrupt the conversation. That was the deal.

The larger pubs had PA systems, and it wasn't unusual to find someone on the mic leading a chorus of Irish standards like "Paddy Reilly," "Fields of

Athenry," and "Danny Boy." Everyone would join in the anthem to sing along with the rebel songs and tales of woe that showcased the Irish spirit. We were unified in celebrating Ireland, joining in with the Irish struggle with our voices.

Such venues were leaderless town halls—at least, the only leader was the bartender. They served up drinks as the community ministered to themselves in their views, their politics, their observations on the human condition.

We had little, yet everyone had enough when we came together for *cois tine*. There was no sense sitting around complaining when there was so much to do together. Everyone left with some more insight about what's sacred to the whole town and what their part in it is.

Whether in the home or pub, I could never tell who was actually a blood relative, but it turned out it didn't matter. The ones who were family showed themselves. True, the family wasn't always functioning well, but it was never dull.

Later, I came to understand the expression *neil aon tinteán mar do thinteán féin*— "There's no fireside like your own." Put another way—there's no more important sacred space than the one you create within yourself. This is where your own truth lives.

Yet this lesson evaded me for years. The pain I faced in my upbringing would pull a veil over the beautiful blending of elements in the *cois tine*. It was a concept that I would forsake, waiting to be reclaimed.

I grew up thinking that politics was the stuff of the elite and the rich. Little did I know how politics permeated so much of my own experience. Even then, I believed that nobody should die for their politics but that the politicians surely needed to create environments that were safe for us to disagree and make our cases known—to facilitate *cois tine* on a larger scale.

The struggle was real. Downtrodden Irish Catholics were coming into their own, consuming just enough from the outside world to know what was possible—while preserving an identity and morality that were birthrights bestowed to all born on the island. A right to be fed from the land, defend the land, and stand up for what was right.

Somber and melancholy at times, uproarious and defiant, we stood up for the national anthem at the end of every large gathering, never forgetting that the fight for freedom was ours. Fight we would—even if it meant separation amongst us on the island.

The truth is, I didn't understand. I didn't want to fight. I wanted to believe that by simply spreading love and peace, the cycles of violence would end.

Eventually, the violence did end, and Ireland became a modern democracy of peace and dreams all of our own—to show the world that on this tiny island in the most western part of Europe, the West was indeed "awake" as Mary Robinson, a former leader of Ireland, said in her inauguration speech. We were awake to the moral obligation to live up to the principles of freedom that we had fought for.

For my part, I didn't see a path in politics, so I took to the skies and decided to leave behind the trauma of being "downtrodden" and make my own way in the world, by lining my bank account and using the power of the almighty dollar to connect myself to the world. Little did I know that my own politics were already deeply sown and until I could reconcile all of this, no amount of wealth could heal me from exposure to the demons that I had come to know, many of them creations of my own design.

SCARS

At eleven months old, I spent five weeks in the hospital. As the oldest child in the family, it was just me with my mother and grandfather. Ma was making lunch for my father, where my grandfather was also in the kitchen at the time, as I sat in my toddler chair.

Ma had set the kettle to boil in an electric jug, the cord swinging down near my highchair. At some point, I reached up, grabbed the cord, and pulled it down. It landed on my neck and shoulder, which was only covered by a plastic bib.

In the ensuing panic, my mother told me years later she passed out and had to be resuscitated by my grandfather. Learning this, I asked, "Then who was holding me?"

While I have no conscious memories of the incident, the scar it left behind was my constant companion. In my teen years, it made me feel unattractive and unappealing to boys. I felt as though I could not be beautiful—or like I wasn't a girl at all.

The scar birthed in me the feeling I had to be a strong, survivor type in the world. This sentiment was only deepened by Ma, who would call it, "The proud pieces of your scar." She was referring to the keloids that had formed. But I felt no pride in it. Only shame.

On a soul level, I was also scarred. I felt alone. Untended. Broken.

I did not remain an only child. Before long, I was joined by my three brothers—Don, Shane, and Pascal.

My parents met and married when they were only eighteen—and were wholly unsuited for one another. My mother has always been a stereotypical case of an introvert—shy, withdrawn, introspective, and lacking in social confidence. Her ruling emotion was fear, her personal mantra was, "I don't know where this goes. I'm scared."

For her, I believe the marriage was one of love, but also convenience—and necessity. Here was a man with a union job, working for a utility company.

The paycheck was small, but his dreams were big—backed up by an incisive wit and powerful intellect. She was charmed by my father's intellect, seeing an escape from her own chaotic household. But she never thought at that young age how his intellect could be weaponized against her, to beat her down into an emotional cage.

Indeed, my father was both charismatic and enigmatic as a character. With a slender build and average height, his physical appearance isn't particularly unique. But he knew how to attract attention, standing on his head—a quirk I suppose I inherited as I still enjoy the challenge of a handstand.

He was a chameleon, adapting to his surroundings. In public, he could be the life of the party—funny, brilliant, ready to pick up an instrument and belt out a ballad. He could pick up a pen and harness his inner artist, bringing forth still life drawings from blank pages and creating animations as handily as he could tile a bathroom or lay flooring. Meanwhile, at home, he was withdrawn, lost in his thoughts, and emotionally unavailable.

Except for the anger. The anger was ever-present. He was one who had to always be right. He could not abide an argument and held a very black and white view of the world—a contradiction in his nature as he accused the Church of being too rigid, which was his excuse for staying away from mass except for the high sacraments. He viewed the Catholic Church as a "straitjacket" for people like himself. He thought himself more free-spirited and enlightened than he truly was.

His frame may have been average, but his physical bearing became animated when he had to rage and yell cruel things, the glare off his spectacles like furious sparks. And when yelling was not enough, there was always the belt, though he preferred to use his hand with me. One time, he beat me for so long, my mother kept shouting for him to stop—one of the few times I saw her stand up to him. Not that it worked.

Reading was my escape. From an early age, I was an avid reader, giving myself sore eyes from reading under the covers late into the night.

In my imagination, I could disappear. First, in the words of Enid Blyton and the *Bunty* books. But then in a bookcase in the furnished home we bought in Mullingar, I picked up Voltaire for the first time and began to ingest other books which I didn't quite yet understand but found fascinating.

Where others would praise my brilliance and comment on "what a great talker" I was, Ma complained constantly of how exhausting it was "to put up" with me, even accusing me of giving my brother a stutter when he was young. Why? Because I would use my voice to defend him when he couldn't find his own.

"I don't know where she came from," she would say to others, as if I were not there to hear her. To my face, she would say, "You think too many things, Gráinne."

She saw intelligence in a girl as a curse. It was one I was glad to bear, at least until she would add, "You're just like your father."

My intelligence came from my father, yet how could anything good come from him? Attributing my intelligence to him has been difficult, knowing the oppression she felt at his hands, as though oppression was the destiny of anyone learned and observant. A belief that the brilliant use their power to crush those less gifted. It crushed me to realize she felt my very existence might turn her into a "victim" of a darker power. Thus, my own mind was the mirror of the monster I had to face.

Growing up In the 1970's—with parents born in the 1950's—scarcity was real. You could *feel* the lack. The Troubles in Northern Ireland were also real and presented a significant challenge for those of us who wanted a united island, but did not want to use a gun to achieve it. It was complicated and difficult to hold these notions of patriotism, national identity, and indigenous culture in a country torn and scarred by violence.

My father had benefited from foreign direct investment into the country and had made his way out of the poverty of his own upbringing.

From the ranks of a working-class electrician in overalls to a manager in a suit, he began working for an international pharmaceutical company, Abbott.

Yet this upward social mobility would cause significant disruption to our home lives as his increasing absence only heightened his struggle to be a father to four young children at home. Not when he could operate as an international man of mystery on the American stage, bringing back the occasional Pez dispenser or other American novelty as trite peace offerings.

Looking back, I can see how his pain was taken out on us through violence, abandonment, and a disassociation from his "old life" in rural Ireland. His identity crisis formed a significant imprint, a scar, on my own experience—though I didn't fully understand this until my healing journey.

You may not even be aware of how your own scars got there. I have no memory of the scalding incident—just the story that has been shared with me. I could not see how my father's scars were also becoming my own. It would take decades for me to uncover them.

Perhaps my mother, despite her faults, was correct on that count—maybe we do need to look at the "proud pieces" of our scars. Perhaps it is in our imperfections that we can find true beauty and strength. When we cover up our scars, though, we allow the wound to fester in our mind, body, and spirit.

As a child, though, I was deeply angry about how my mother "othered" me for being a girl who was "too ahead of herself." Years later, I would learn how, yes, indeed, I needed to first put my own pain down. The logical and intellectual mind could not save me from the fear inside—the fear I would become a force of darkness.

Years later, I told her, "You will always be safe with me. I have no need to fight and no thirst for revenge against this world. My very existence is enough. No weapon, no shield."

The enemy I fight today is not my father—the ghost of a man I haven't seen in decades living under my bed, nor the "Jekyll and Hyde" that turned into someone else in a fit of rage, still taking up space in my head. Rather, the enemy in me is the belief that I need any power from anywhere other than the beat of my own heart and the depth of my own spirit. The truth has no charge when it lands, no power. It just exists.

STAGES

As The Troubles turned our eyes to America, stories would come back of the riches of America. This was further accented by the glamor of Hollywood and the Kennedys. My Uncle Noel introduced me to the incisively clever slapstick of the Marx Brothers, the fantasy of Disney films like *Mary Poppins*, and I watched *The Wizard of Oz* on repeat, seeing it as the story of life itself—going on a journey to find your way home.

Like many cultures, the Irish have a special relationship to storytelling. As a child, I was immersed in our folklore and was even called upon to read the old stories in front of the class because I was one of the few who could do so in the ancient tongue.

When I was ten years old, we were pulled from the *cois tine* of our community in Tullamore when my father accepted a new job in Donegal, a town on the northwest coast, near the border of Northern Ireland. Few outsiders lived in Donegal—it was the type of place where the ancestries of its citizens stretched back beyond memory.

With its cultural proximity to Scotland, it also stood as unique among Irish towns. For generations, the Scots and Irish had enjoyed commerce across the water and adopted each other's traits. Yet with our purely Irish accents and sensibilities, this only made us stand out more. It was like being an immigrant in my own country—an experience which would end up preparing me for my own immigration later.

The saving grace of the move was the thriving children's theatre in Donegal, which was a combined effort of the girls' convent school and the boys' school. All my young life, there was an artist in me wanting to come out—and yet too scared to do so. But if I was going to stick out like a sore thumb, then I figured I might as well embrace it.

I had no understanding back then that, as the protector of my brothers, I was already losing my Divine Feminine energy at so young an age. In standing up to my father in their defense, I had to learn to play a part—to adopt a mask of masculinity to match his own toxic variety.

Now on the stage, I would have a healthy outlet for such a mask. And as fate would have it, the first play I auditioned for was Hansel and Gretel, and I was cast as Hansel.

Yes, you read that correctly; I was put in the boys' role. Mind you, there were boys who auditioned for the role, yet the sisters chose to give it to me instead, possibly because I've always had a deeper voice compared to my female peers.

At first, I thought it was extremely cool to be playing a boy—it would really give me the chance to perform. Then somewhere inside myself, a voice objected, saying, "But you're a girl, Gráinne!"

But the voice was too similar to my mother's, so I hushed it. I wanted to play the leading role. I wanted to be at the center of the story. Today, I wonder if this voice was actually the Divine Feminine within, speaking to me, cautioning me against losing my identity.

After Hansel, I landed another leading role, this time in *Peter Pan*. This was less of a gender issue for me, as the role of Peter is traditionally played by a woman. But the issue I found was that the costume was so short, I had a personal modesty crisis over how many tights I could wear so that people wouldn't see my legs.

By this time, I was going through puberty—my body was changing, and so I now felt more at odds with playing the male. But I still wanted to be the star. Like a cruel joke of the universe, I had my period during the show. And because I was unprepared and had nothing to absorb the flow, I had to go change my clothes. Yet the show must go on?

The irony isn't lost on me—to have such a visceral moment of growing up while pretending to be the Boy Who Never Grows Up. It's the perfect analogy for the existential crisis I would face through the next several decades as I would put on costume after costume, trying to find the right fit, forsaking my feminine energy for the masculine mask.

I've always been drawn to the costumes in theatre and film. The colors, the festivity, the eccentricity of it all. The only vestige of my theatre days is how I choose to dress myself, as I still use clothes as a way to express myself.

Performing had been a means of survival. It was a bright spot of my childhood as even my parents supported me in it and would come to my shows, as surprising as this may be. It had been a healthy outlet for my need to be seen, the natural desire to be celebrated. Yet I also took from it a dangerous lesson—to be celebrated, I could not be myself. I needed to become someone else. I needed the costume and mask to be loved.

So as I moved into my teens and my non-conforming ways only increased, the artist within me was suffocated by fear—specifically the fear of money. All the artists I knew were unconventional geniuses—but poor. The first, I could live with. The poverty part, I could not.

For many years, I dwelled on the notion that the only way out was to use the intelligence I was given. I could leverage my intellectual mind to excel in the world, making money the only measure of productivity that mattered. Somehow, in my mind, I believed that the only way to be free was to have a high-paying job and to be defined by this, more than anything else.

After all, the "Brain Drain" of Ireland was in full force throughout my childhood, and many of our brightest minds emigrated to the US. If my intelligence was a curse in Ireland, then perhaps it could transform into a blessing in America. Perhaps only on the grand stage of Western capitalism could I heal the scars I bore.

ESCAPES

Growing up in the 1970s in Ireland, I was constantly reminded that our world was painted with the hues of adventure and exploration. We didn't need streetlights to guide us home—the dawn's first light signaled the end of our nocturnal escapades.

Home was painfully binary—a cage of conflict. To escape this, my days were filled with roaming the earth, feeling as one with nature, and embracing the changing rhythms of life.

We spent endless hours outdoors, basking in the sun, moon, and stars. With no cars or buses, we relied on our own two feet to carry us home, taking in the sights and sounds of the neighborhood along the way.

We'd pop into neighbors' homes unannounced, welcomed with open arms and lively conversations that danced around the circle of life. These were my true homes—where I was accepted and loved and cherished. The home where my parents were was more akin to a hotel—a place for eating and sleeping. And if I never had to do either of those, perhaps I would never go home.

Sitting by the fireside or gathered around the kitchen table, we shared stories and laughter, cherishing the simplicity of our surroundings—*cois tine*. We foraged for wild berries and sampled nature's bounty, relishing the earthy flavors of potatoes and carrots fresh from the soil.

In Donegal, the ocean was our playground, its waves calling to us with an irresistible allure. We learned to read the signs of the tide as we searched for barnacles and crabs in low tide and felt the pull of the current, the thrill of sand swirling between our toes when the tide rushed back in.

Even as jellyfish and other creatures of the sea reminded us of Mother Nature's power, we reveled in all her wonders.

Summer days brought sun-kissed skin and the occasional insect bite, but nothing could dampen our spirits. We crafted makeshift toys from whatever we could find, turning everyday objects into vessels of imagination and joy. We fished without rods, surfed without boards, and swam in our clothes. Childlike innovation of the highest order.

Despite the simplicity of our surroundings, our lives were rich with sound and song. Whether it was the clatter of kitchen spoons or the haunting melody of a harp or a tin whistle, we found music in the everyday moments of life.

Through it all, we learned to be resourceful, to find beauty in simplicity, and to cherish the connections that bind us to one another and to the natural world.

My childhood adventures taught me valuable lessons about the natural world that continue to shape my life today more than ever. When I have authentic conversations from the heart and when my feet are on the natural earth, I find myself transported—*cois tine*. These escapes were one side of the coin.

The reality is that there was another strand woven into my young life experience from the history of the country I was born in. A country that had been transformed by British colonization, famine, and challenges to the traditional way of life.

Livelihoods were dominated by agriculture and the dominance of the Catholic religion, both of which were under threat from all directions, including internal. The impact was everywhere—not only the economy, but deeper into culture and ideology, and what a modern Ireland could represent to both the world and its citizens. In the wake of globalization and modernization, Ireland has lost much of its *cois tine* spirit. I meet few younger Irish people who know the term and what all it entails.

With my grades, education offered the first step in escape—and what better way to make money than to learn how to make money?

The first step in my escape plan meant applying for any international program I could while I was in school. I wanted to learn international finance and the technological systems enabling it. I longed for a world that was interconnected—especially for myself.

After a stint in Belgium, the first cracks in my escape plan began to show. I had successfully avoided crossing paths with my father for an entire year, but now I had to make a trip home. Nothing had changed. Not that I had expected it to.

"I'm not paying to send you back there," he railed, face flushed, hands clenched.

Seething with the cruelty of his words, I pulled on the metaphorical helmet for battle. "You don't need to," I retorted. "I have my own money to pay my way."

I wanted the words to slice him. And perhaps they did. But I can't be sure because I stormed out and went to party with my friends, whiling away the hours with drink and dance, intoxicating my senses.

When I got home late, I found the door to my room open. The Auld Man was sitting there, waiting.

"I'm leaving your ma," he announced. "I have a place to go that's safe."

What did I care if he was safe or not? As far as I was concerned, this was the best news I'd heard from him.

"Good, be gone," I answered. "Why are you still here?"

His eyes met mine. I'm not sure why he said what he said next, but maybe it was the smell of alcohol on me.

"Your grandmother died an alcoholic," he said. "When she died, I went to the coffin where she lay, and one of her eyes was opened. When I closed it, I said to her, 'I'm glad your suffering is over.'"

I stood there, stunned, wondering to myself, *Why is he telling me this? Does he think he's a martyr of divine suffering? Am I supposed to feel sorry for him? And what about me, who deeply loved my grandmother whose memory he was daring to sully?* I thought I couldn't be any more disgusted by him than I already was.

Until his next words:

"When you were a tiny child and got scalded," he said calmly, "I must have decided then I could not love you. What happened, it was too sore, too painful."

Heat surged through me, new pain tearing through my soul, scarring me anew. How could this man be so fixated on his own pain and not see the damage he had inflicted on me for eighteen years? How could he not see the pain he was inflicting now with his words?

29

Or perhaps he did know. Perhaps this was his twisted form of revenge for saying I did not need him. Either way, I wanted nothing more than to get away. So I did.

Shortly after my return to Belgium, he told Ma his plan for leaving her. My brothers told me how he jumped out the window—not the door—and never came back for his belongings. For us, it was cause for celebration.

Ma came to visit me in her grief and to console herself at my side. "My husband left me. I'm all alone, and it's terrible," she lamented. And then she said something which seemed at odds with her grief. "He made my life *so* difficult that parts of myself were buried for years."

She was at war with her own pain. For years, I had judged her as weak. Had dismissed her for it. Yes, there had been isolated instances when she had tried to reason with my father, to talk him down, to push back against him. But most of the time, she had sided with him by backing down. Yet I began to realize that maybe she had no choice but to do so. Perhaps she was also his victim. She had thought he was an escape—but he had become her cage, too.

I saw my father once more after that, after he had moved in with his mistress. My brother Pascal was only thirteen at the time and began to struggle with his eyesight—something he had clearly inherited from our father, who was blind as a bat without his spectacles.

Yet instead of assisting Pascal at his eyeglass appointment, he merely drove him to the store and then left. With no one to help him navigate the choices, Pascal came home, distraught over the pair of "geeky," heavy frames he had ended up with. "No one was there to help me," he said. "He dumped me at the door."

I was enraged. "Get in the car now," I ordered everyone. "We're going to see my father."

No one dared disobey. I sat in the passenger seat, silent—my brothers in the backseat as we drove over.

When our father saw us standing there, he grimly uttered, "How dare you come here." And then slammed the door in our faces.

My brother Shane threatened to smash the windows or break the door down if he didn't come back—and believe me, Shane had the frame to do so. He was always more of a gentle giant, but unafraid to use his strength in the moment.

But because I didn't want further hurt, we climbed back in the car and drove off. My brothers were all crying. Ma sat in her seat, helpless. Her only contribution was to verbalize what we already knew: "Your father's a horrible person."

In the following years, I sought to move further and further from my past, further away from my father and the pain he had brought all of us. Nothing and no one would hold me back anymore.

At my first real job in London, I was told I would be held back by two factors: "Being a woman and being Irish."

"Fine," I told myself. "Then I can play whatever part I need to play."

I assumed a mask of masculine energy, silencing the Divine Feminine within me. I minimized my Irish heritage and upbringing, burying the good with the bad, forsaking *cois tine*. When I moved to America and married an American, I thought I had put the final nail in the coffin of my Irish-ness.

Like the story of my father and his mother, it was as if I leaned over the corpse of Irish Gráinne, closed her eyes, and said, "Escape your pain."

Like so many others, I also took to the boat to make my fortune and became part of the American diaspora. I had to escape scarcity for abundance. Yet I was only looking at the external signs of abundance— material possessions and job titles. I did not realize that true abundance must first happen in the mind. And so even as I thought I was escaping scarcity, it remained trapped within me.

I left my homeland behind, thinking this was the key to escape—but I brought myself with me. Hard as you may try, you can never escape yourself.

FREEDOM

In an interview with journalist Bill Moyers, American poet and civil rights activist Maya Angelou addressed the question of freedom:

"You only are free when you realize you belong to no place—you belong to every place—no place at all."

"Do you belong to anyone?" Moyers followed up.

"More and more … I belong to myself."

Freedom from pain can only be found when we accept that pain belongs to us. When we cross the darkness to find the light within us. When we acknowledge that pain is the discussion we must first have with ourselves.

I realized in the writing of this book that when I speak of my father, I talk of him as though he were dead. Yet at the time I'm writing this, he is still alive—still living in Ireland, though I have had no contact with him in decades.

When I look back now, I suspect my father had deep pain—which he then projected onto all of us, forcing us to absorb it. He was an incredibly artistic individual with a brilliant mind. And yet he could not be the man he wanted to be because of his own circumstances—the abuse he had faced at the hands of his own belligerent father who had driven my grandmother into alcoholism.

In many ways, this makes my father a parable—a lesson in what happens when you don't let your pain belong to you. When you force it onto others. It does not diminish—but grows like an infection.

That's not to say you stifle the pain either. But the first step in freedom is to realize that it cannot be found in a place. I never found the freedom I sought in America, nor in a job title. I moved from corporation to corporation, swimming with the sharks of Wall Street, and yet freedom always eluded me.

My failure to face my own pain contributed to my eventual divorce, which then spread pain to my three children and to my ex-husband, no doubt.

This came to the forefront when I tried talk therapy with a therapist accomplished in the Jungian method. When I shared with him the story of confronting my father over Pascal's glasses, he made an observation: "Sounds like you were there for your mother and your brothers. But who was there for you?"

No one. But how could that help me now? He brought me back to those experiences, which only served to re-traumatize me.

At the end of the session, he said, "Okay, Ms. McNamara, we need to deal with your father, the man in Donegal, and your father, the monster in your head."

While this was incredibly insightful, it provided me with no healing. Some people find talk therapy essential in their healing journey. But I felt like my ribcage had been ripped open, exposing my beating heart—and nothing had been done to cauterize the wound. I was sent out into the world with no idea of what to do with the pain bleeding out of me.

Still, the experience taught me an essential truth about finding freedom from your pain: The answers are inside you.

It's really uncomfortable to face them, but if you can stay there in the discomfort, you will find the light.

If you have the capacity to be triggered by the past, as I was, then you have to find a way to go there safely to heal. Perhaps for you it will be talk therapy. For me, plant healing is what safely opened me up to cross the darkness and find the light.

Because the light inside me all along was the fireside of cois tine. You don't get the warmth of the fire without inhaling the smoke. In trying to find freedom from the pain of my upbringing, I had tried to escape the beautiful parts, too. I had divorced the core pieces of myself in trying to form a new identity.

Cois tine is the fireside ritual you need to have with yourself. It requires you to stop, sit, and have the important discussions with yourself. It can be chaotic and noisy at times—but it can also fill you with harmony if you let it.

By holding cois tine within myself, I pulled back the veil on the relationship between my trauma, anxiety and depression, and my addictions. I quit drinking, which had been my way to numb the pain, and began the real process of healing from within.

Doing so has taken me all the way back to who I really am at the core. Back to the little girl sitting on her grandmother's lap to feel the heat from the fire, or finding a candy in the pocket of her cardigan for me.

My natural state is one of kindness and compassion. When others suffer, I want to help bring an end to their suffering. But for decades, I allowed the fear of my own shame to hold me back from being the person I wanted to be. I stifled the artist within, only letting her out in my wardrobe through a keen fashion sensibility.

Despite a deep connection to spirituality, I mostly hid this in the workplace. I'm curious, talkative, and social, yet I also need time alone—if for no other reason than to reconnect to conduct the ritual of cois tine within me.

In my healing journey, I've been able to study aspects of many cultures, traveling far and wide to understand the history of our future as people. With deep respect for all forms of indigenous spiritual practices and healing methods, I've found that cois tine is not a purely Irish concept at all. Every culture has its own version of the fireside discussion, the search for meaning in the mundane, and novelty to share.

As a ritual, cois tine represents the coming together of various energies, integrating as a unifying beam of light. But when that energy is out of sync, it creates discord—with yourself and others.

Many mistakes have been made in my life, and I have placed myself and others in danger as a result. I have had darkness in me when my own exposed vulnerability has been exploited for the gain of others.

Every day is a new exercise in healing so that I can choose love. When the darkness comes, I count on my own intuition to guide.

I've come to know that what I craved from others in the past are the very things I was denying myself. Freedom. Truth. Forgiveness. Kindness. Peace. Dignity. Respect. Generosity. Love.

But when we join in the ritual of cois tine, then the kingdom of heaven is here. "Love thy neighbor as thyself." How can you love your neighbor if you do not love yourself?

The human consciousness has to make sense of all the data it has ingested—to uncover how our experiences are connected to everything else. Only then can the path chosen have resonance and coherence.

In these intimate, cois tine moments, we must know ourselves. We have to do the work to know what's true for us in our own souls and what our own worth is. Our worth is not in material possessions but in the spirit.

Not everyone is brave enough to do the work—but anyone can be brave enough. The price of freedom is being fearless indeed. There are no pockets in the shrouds. You must make sure you share your spirit with the people that you meet. Your legacy can then be left in the world, not to people you name in a will. Otherwise, you confuse value with worth and will forever chase the latter.

As Irish poet Oscar Wilde so kindly put it, "Experience is the hardest kind of teacher. It gives you the test first and the lesson afterward." I got the lesson ten times over until I understood I was taking a test. I simply had not done the work. Parts of me were still unexplored. You'll likely find the same—and one day it will all make sense.

Narrative is humanity's most defining framework. The stories we tell ourselves matter far more than the blows of life or the words we absorb from the world. Especially if your story has been one of hard knocks. Narrative is critical—how you interpret your relationship with yourself, with the world, and with others.

The following chapters will each be cois tine rituals—sacred conversations held with the women I've met on my healing journey. In each story, you'll see the fireside conversation that had to first happen within. You'll see the narratives of how each woman came from a place of pain, faced the darkness, and channeled the energy within her to vibrate with herself to elevate mind, body, and spirit.

It is this energy of freedom and wholeness which allows us to connect, to hold cois tine rituals with one another. It's how we rotate from pain to healing, from emptiness to wholeness.

Not everyone can take the same journey to freedom, nor do we need to. Each of us has different starting points. Not everyone can walk away from their lives and their jobs to take spiritual tours, but as we will discover in the following chapters, the journey home to self is more critical than ever. As we enter into an era of unprecedented abstraction and disambiguation, where the human experience is being reduced to algorithms, we must learn to see what is true.

Life brought me and these other women to the point where we can be emissaries to help point the way. Your journey to the fireside will cover different terrain and involve different obstacles. But in our collective consciousness, we can find the universal strands of truth that unite us.

Looking ahead, we must begin with the mind. We must rotate it from a place of scarcity and victimhood to a place of brave exploration. How?

First, pray. Prayer is not about a call to a specific deity, though you are welcome to do so in alignment with your own faith. Instead, prayer is about engaging your mind to refocus on gratitude.

I think of gratitude as merci, the French word for "thanks." I recognize the gift of being alive in this moment and have "mercy" for what is to come, that which has not yet been revealed. In this mercy, I can know the protection of the divine, the Creator, the Source. In my own journey back from agnostic belief, I have found resolute acceptance that there is a higher power that is indeed Almighty.

Next, play. Engage your body, open yourself to new experiences, to new ideas, so long as you do not stray from your personal ethics, beliefs, and boundaries. Explore healing methods to find the right fit for you. But please do so from a place of caution, not recklessness. Then join with others—sing, dance, paint, swim, run—whatever play looks like for you, embrace its healing power.

And then finally, create. Use your experiences from pray and play to stir up your spirit. From the overflow of healing, you will find abundance to create new opportunities, new insights, new tools that allow you to connect the light within yourself, to vibrate the energy into a stream of joy.

All three are the essence of cois tine—in deep discussions, we engaged our minds, with our talents, we engaged our bodies, and in the creation of art, we lifted our spirits.

When we gathered for cois tine, the fears of home and scarcity vanished. There was only abundance, safety, and freedom.

Lose yourself. Find yourself. Find others.

It's time to Rotate. Ready yourself. Pray. Play. Create.

CHAPTER 3

TEACHERS AND HEALERS

My story nearly ended at thirteen.

Another day, another screaming match with my father, my brothers as onlookers. My screams were a pushback on his aggression, but I'm certain I looked like a crazy person. I *felt* like a crazy person. The moment was an out-of-body experience—and a voice of dark energy saying, "You *are* crazy. You are the problem. You don't belong here."

I couldn't argue with the voice. The reality I was living seemed to confirm, "I don't belong here. This is the wrong scene. I'm not supposed to be in this movie."

So many nights leading up to this fight, I'd come home from friends' houses, experiencing a taste of their lives—and realize just how broken our home was. The loneliness of it crushed me. I'd fight back the tears in bed, desperate to escape.

Had the resources been available, I wouldn't be surprised if I had been diagnosed as clinically depressed. But there was no way to get such a diagnosis in rural, sea-battered Donegal.

And since no one ever talked about depression, I had no way to qualify what I was feeling, no way to question these thoughts. In that moment, the pain *was* reality.

For years, I had made it my job not to *feel*. Unable to escape the inevitable pain, I decided to take the next step: to never feel any pain ever again.

I took a box full of over-the-counter painkillers, swallowed a fistful of pills, and plunged into the darkness. Both literal and figurative.

Life was a nightmare I did not want to wake up from. This was the only escape I saw before me.

When I awoke, the first sight I can remember was of my father standing over me. If ever there was a moment for compassion, for reconciliation, this was it.

"You'll have to take more than that to finish the job," he taunted. "Keep it up and we're going to put you into a mental home. Is that what you want?"

The dark energy spoke again:

"See? It's you. You're the problem."

But as strange as it sounds, that attempt became the seed of my first great lesson: *You are not broken. You don't hate yourself. You hate what you are feeling inside because you feel alone.* That clarity—faint as a candle in the dark—would return again and again in my life, reminding me that healing is never about "fixing" what is broken, but about remembering wholeness is possible. And decades later, it was that same lesson that greeted me again at the banks of the Ganges in India.

EARLY SEEDS OF FAITH AND HEALING

Growing up in the Catholic Church, I'd always been captivated by the stories of the Roman Catholic church. I'd seen the priests as extraordinary performers—they knew their lines and spoke them with such flair and drama in Tullamore.

In Donegal, the priests were more subdued, and the more modern church I attended was built in the "round" style like a theatre, not a cathedral. The Latin and lace and burning incense were remarkably captivating and theatrical to me. So too were the practices of kneeling and standing, and in particular the art of *genuflection* before entering the pew. It was almost impossible not to be performative while maintaining an ounce of grace in this particular act of reverence on bended knee.

While I no longer identify as Catholic, I'd always loved the gospels and parables—and the conversations I could have with God and the saints through prayer. There had always been a profound mystery to it all, a channel into something deep and eternal. In those experiences were the acorns of my later discovery of meditation.

In the biblical stories, one can see the hints of the true nature of healing—that healing must come from within. When the gospels describe Christ's miracles, specifically when he heals someone, he never says, "I have healed you." No—rather, he says, "Your *faith* has healed you."

Your faith. An energy that resides within you, ready to burst forth from the doubt and pain that seeks to suffocate it.

In the wake of surviving the suicide attempt, I decided to attend a Church-run retreat for other troubled teens. Though the years have wiped away much of what happened during the retreat, I can still recall reading letters that others had written to me. They were love letters from other broken souls—words of both pain and comfort, proof that I was not alone. Although I recall feeling deep vulnerability, reading about the strength and compassion they saw in me was comforting. More importantly, it was authentic. Experiencing the pain of others hurt me a great deal, and it was all too easy to ignore my own pain and focus on everyone else's.

Even though I was moving away from the Church's teaching by then, here I had found a community of peers opening up about their own struggles with the darkness—and a glimpse of the light.

The retreat gave me the first sign that healing is possible and that the faith to heal comes from within. When you are surrounded by others who support you in the quest for healing, you can begin to access those frequencies of healing—faith, love, and hope.

But it would take decades for me to connect the dots via a divine appointment with fellow travelers in India.

Gráinne McNamara

A PORTAL CALLED RISHIKESH

While on my healing journey in 2022, and after firing myself from my lofty corporate career, I found my way to an ashram in Rishikesh, India. I had decided to research the roots of yoga and take a month of yoga teacher training. To say it was a "vibe shift" would be an understatement. Ashrams are monasteries with deep spiritual significance, so between the setting and the yoga, we were combining the energy of mind, body, and spirit.

The ashram in Rishikesh was nothing glamorous—basic vegetarian meals served in repetition, chai masala as a small treat, cows wandering freely through the living quarters, and monkeys who became bold and aggressive around mealtimes. The Himalayas rose like ancient guardians behind us, while the Ganges below maintained its eternal flow, carrying stories and sorrows downstream.

My room was simple, my shower broken, and yet I was grateful to have it to myself when most had to share. On the first morning, I bundled up against the cold predawn air and stepped into the studio for the 6:00 a.m. mantra session.

The group gathered silently, waiting. We waited ... and waited. No teacher arrived.

At the top of the hour, the next instructor for the asana practice appeared, and without explanation, we carried on as though nothing had happened.

Inside, I was fuming. How could they disrespect us like this? Who was in charge? Why hadn't anyone told us?

Later, at lunch, I marched to the office to confront the man who ran the center, as he was listed in the program as the leader of the chanting.

"Is everything okay?" I asked, masking my irritation.

"Yes," he replied calmly. "Everything is fine. Two students arrived in the middle of the night. I stayed up to welcome them and fell asleep afterward. I was tired."

His words landed with a thud. Everything was fine. He hadn't "failed" us. There was no scandal.

The "hierarchy" I'd assumed—a teacher above students, authority above seekers—was made up. And the truth was embarrassingly simple: my expectations had created a story in my mind only. This self-concocted "drama" and assumption of disrespect had taken my focus away from where it should have been. I'd spent the entirety of the morning wondering why others did not share my indignation at being stood up on a cold morning thousands of miles from home. That moment of humility was the real beginning of my training. Not in asana, not in philosophy— but in letting go.

That was the lesson. No apology, no justification. Just truth, simple and uncluttered. In that exchange, I received perhaps the greatest teachings of the entire training about letting go:

1. Hierarchy is made up.

2. Expectations lead to suffering.

This wasn't New York where Wall Street bulls snort at the slightest delay. This was Hari Om. The vibration here was peace, not performance. And so began my journey into removing everything from myself that was not my own so that I could shift to my authentic vibration.

The backdrop of Rishikesh mirrored the yoga lessons in its own chaotic beauty. During free time we ventured into the village to buy "energy balls" made of amaranth and nuts. And we visited local tailors who could make beautiful outfits from fabric bought at the markets.

My favorite outings, though, were to the banks of the Ganges. The sacred river, glacial and immense, was a flowing reminder that time and truth are larger than we are. At dusk, the river itself became a temple. Locals and pilgrims gathered for a ritual called Ganga Aarti, setting small leaf bowls afloat, each holding a flickering candle and bright marigolds.

The water carried away these visible prayers—flames trembling, yet unextinguished, weaving light into the current. I watched in silence, surrounded by strangers and tourists alike, feeling that resonance of devotion: not to a god outside us, but to the eternal flow that carries us all.

Likewise, the people in the yoga program became their own kind of mirror. Two young ladies classically trained as ballerinas showed breathtaking grace on the mat yet broke down in tears during pranayama. They both discovered how their years of training had taught them to hold their bellies flat, never expanding, never breathing deeply. The freedom of the belly's rise and fall cracked them open in ways no pose ever could.

Inside, I allowed myself to breathe more deeply and I too noticed how uncommon this was for me. I had also struggled with digestive issues for my whole life because of my inability to "access" or relax my abdominal area and sensitivity to processed foods.

One afternoon, we were visited by a renowned Ayurvedic doctor, a man whose training straddled both Eastern and Western medicine. He spoke with gentle authority about balance, digestion, and the subtle ways our bodies speak long before disease sets in. He then invited us each to his clinic for a dosha assessment.

In Ayurveda, doshas are patterns of energy that reflect our constitution; our habits, behaviors, and sensitivities. Vata, associated with air and movement, tends toward creativity but also anxiety and restlessness when out of balance. Pitta, aligned with fire, fuels drive and clarity but can tip into anger or inflammation. Kapha, connected to earth and water, brings stability and compassion. However, when excessive, it may become lethargy or attachment. Most of us are a blend, but understanding our dominant dosha is like being handed a map of our tendencies. It is a way to see where harmony can be restored.

What stayed with me most, though, was one simple sentence the doctor shared: "In the West, food is judged by its shelf life. In Ayurveda, it is judged by its cell life."

That phrase cracked something open in me. How much of what I was eating was inert, lifeless—packaged for convenience, designed for preservation, not nourishment?

I began to see food not just as fuel, but as vibration, carrying either vitality or stagnation into my cells. A "sattvic" diet in yogic philosophy and Ayurveda is one that promotes clarity, harmony and balance. In my case, my diet has shifted toward more fresh fruits and vegetables, nuts and seeds and local and seasonal produce from green grocers and farmers markets. I pared back in other areas to make space in my budget for the premium this food required. It was an investment not in my pantry, but in my own vitality.

Ayurveda also offered me tools for my lifelong digestive struggles. I began taking triphala, a gentle herbal blend that has supported motility and soothed discomfort without the harsh side effects of pharmaceuticals. Later, when I traveled to Kerala, the birthplace of Ayurveda, I experienced its healing arts more fully: panchakarma treatments that reset my digestion, and shirodhara, a steady stream of warm oil poured over the third eye, which left me lighter, clearer, and more open in thought.

What struck me most was how participatory it all felt. Unlike the passive model of medicine I had grown up with—waiting for a doctor to prescribe, to diagnose, to intervene—Ayurveda asked me to notice, to align, to take responsibility. It was not a pill, but a practice. And in this practice, I learned what it means to honor the body as a teacher: subtle, wise, and always orienting me back toward balance. With the right guidance, we can heal ourselves naturally.

THE BODY IS A TEACHER

In between the formal yoga training sessions, a recovering addict from England became our group's heartbeat. Carrying his guitar, he strummed, sang, and invited us to gather between classes. He learned the mantras by heart and was always the first to arrive for morning meditation, drawn to the rhythm of sound as if it alone could steady his nervous system. For him, music wasn't just art, it was medicine.

In his presence, I saw how healing was not a performance, but a resonance. For me, it reminded me that music is not separate from us- we are instruments too. Our bones, tissues, and breath form a body that can hum in discord or resonate in harmony. Healing is not about importing something from outside but about learning to tune ourselves, the way he tuned the guitar before playing. And when we are tuned, we don't just live- we vibrate.

Another striking figure in our group was Volker, a therapist who arrived with a graveness that bordered on severity—intense, upright, eyes sharp with inquiry. In our philosophy sessions, we were introduced to the *Yoga Sutras of Patanjali* and the *Vedas*—texts that have shaped spiritual teaching in India for thousands of years.

For many of my peers like Volker, trained in the Western canon of thought, this was unfamiliar ground. They knew Freud and Jung, whose models dissect the psyche into layers of unconscious drives and archetypes. But the *Vedas* offer a different kind of map: one that places consciousness itself, not the ego, at the center. The *Yoga Sutras*, in turn, distill this into a practical framework—ethical guidelines, practices of breath and focus, ways of quieting the fluctuations of the mind so that one can glimpse the self beyond thought. In that stillness, what emerges is not another external authority but the teacher and the healer within-the presence that knows what we need, and has always been waiting for us to listen.

For a Western audience, the significance is profound. We are used to approaching the mind as a problem to be analyzed or solved, often through the lens of pathology. The sutras and the Vedas invite another possibility—that the mind is a doorway, not a puzzle. They suggest that liberation lies not in endless dissection but in stillness, alignment, and direct experience.

During philosophy classes, Volker pushed hard on every point, interrogating the Vedas for evidence and demanding that the sutras justify themselves in terms of measurable outcomes. For him, truth had to pass through reason, and the body was secondary to the mind's dominion.

But as the days unfolded, something shifted. He fell ill, diagnosed with pneumonia, and his breath became shallow, labored. Suddenly, the body he had treated as an instrument of will refused to obey. While the rest of us sat upright in meditation, he lay beneath a yoga blanket in the resting pose called *śavāsana*, struggling to breathe. His questions grew softer, less argumentative. His presence became less about mastering philosophy and more about surrendering into vulnerability.

What struck me most was not his illness but the tenderness it drew from the group. Where once he had been the sharp skeptic, now he was the fragile reminder that no philosophy is lived until it touches the body. The Vedas and sutras no longer seemed abstract—they were living texts, written in the language of breath and limitation. His struggle became a mirror for all of us: that the pursuit of knowledge without embodiment can only take you so far. Sometimes wisdom begins when the mind yields and the body teaches.

Others cracked open in subtler ways. One woman giggled uncontrollably through anatomy class until her laughter dissolved into tears when the teacher questioned her sincerity. Trauma stored in her body found release through movement. No substances, no gurus—just her body remembering itself. That too was teaching. That too was healing.

I began to understand more deeply: yoga is not merely a practice of poses, or breath, or philosophy. It is a portal. Each limb—*asana, pranayama, mantra*, meditation—offers a way in. But the destination is not a teacher's approval, nor an external sign of achievement. The destination is the self, vibrating with its own truth. The meaning of these practices is not in their textbook definitions, it's in the experience of them.

Decades of practice taught me that asana, the movements of yoga, are not about flexibility or postures for their own sake, but about listening to the wisdom the body holds. Sometimes that wisdom comes through resistance. Why do I hold my breath when I fold forward and feel tension in my hamstrings? When I bring my awareness there, I learn that an exhale can send oxygen into the muscles, but also calm my nervous system.

Working the kinks out of the body makes it easier to sit quietly, to rest in stillness.

Pranayama, breathwork, deepened that lesson. Simple patterns like box breathing—in for four counts, hold for four counts, out for four counts, hold for four—teach me presence. My attention drops out of future plans and lands right here, in this inhale, this exhale. And off the mat, when life overwhelms, I have this tool always with me.

Mantra, too, revealed its medicine not through concept but through vibration. The sound of "Om," chanted in a group, reverberates through the chest and body, grounding me, reminding me that I am part of something larger than myself. It is not performance but resonance—an ordering principle that tunes me, like an instrument, to harmony.

Meditation was the most elusive. For years I thought it meant having no thoughts at all, which felt impossible. Then a teacher suggested I imagine my thoughts as butterflies drifting through a breeze—notice them, let them pass, no need to chase or swat them down. This redefined meditation for me as *space in animation*—not absence of thought, but the freedom to witness without attaching, to let thoughts come and go without turning them into stories. Off the mat, that became mindfulness: the capacity to create space, even in the movement of daily life.

Each limb of yoga became a way not just to practice but to heal. They taught me that the healer is not outside me but within—revealed in a stretch, a breath, a sound, or a moment of stillness.

FALSE TEACHERS

It's only human nature to seek out teachers. Our parents are our first teachers—from first steps to first dates, and from first jobs to the first child. We absorb their lessons, for better or worse—those which are spoken and unspoken.

At a certain point, we need new teachers, though. We need to learn from the experience of others to live full lives. As a young girl, my love for school bred in me a desire to be a teacher. And while life took me another direction, I have eventually been able to fulfill that dream, both as an adjunct professor of business strategy and in the opportunities to stand onstage and teach others.

In modern Western society, we have divorced teaching and healing as separate practices. But for most of human history, this has not been the case. Teaching goes hand-in-hand with the healing process. "Self-help" is not truly possible alone. We must learn from those who have gone before us—and pass on the knowledge to the next generation.

Across many of the ancient cultures, you see teaching and healing intricately intertwined. The pharaohs of ancient Egypt received their instruction from the priests who were both healers and teachers. The same occurred in ancient China and in India where healers were also the primary sources of instruction. Likewise, in the tradition of the Hebrews, people sought out the priest for both healing and teaching. In ancient Islamic culture, the scholars were also physicians.

And so the role of shaman can be found in cultures ranging from Asia to Africa to the Americas—individuals who instruct in healing *and* truth. Even up to a couple of hundred years ago, Christian clerics were the ones administering medical care to their local communities, carrying on the ministry of Christ as both healer and teacher.

But in divorcing the concepts of healing and teaching, we have unwittingly created confusion for ourselves. One where we seek healing without seeking to understand the method itself. And when combined with monetization, we have caused a dangerous trend—healing for hire. This creates a Petri dish ready for growing false teachers.

Therefore, we have to ask what happens when your path crosses with a false teacher? What happens when the lesson is fundamentally flawed? What happens when your past trauma blinds you to what is true or false?

It's no surprise that yoga and plant medicine communities often intersect. The idea that we are our own gurus is not new, but often overlooked. And no community is immune to predatory or self-serving behavior. Just because someone is trained in yoga or has experienced plant medicine does not automatically give them the license to administer substances to vulnerable seekers.

At the *ashram*, there was a British woman surreptitiously offering Kambo sessions, approaching students like a recruiter might headhunt for a coveted position. We were sitting cross-legged on the floor, finishing our simple meal, when she began extolling the benefits of her ceremonies. She expounded on the benefits and offered "ceremonies" to anyone interested.

For anyone who hasn't encountered Kambo, it is a traditional Amazonian medicine made from the secretion of a frog, known to trigger intense purging (yes, from both ends!) and sometimes profound emotional release when it's placed on open skin. When done properly, it requires a body that has been prepared for the process, a trained facilitator, and a controlled, supportive environment—set and setting are everything. Here, in a crowded *ashram* dining hall, with no medical support nearby, offering Kambo sessions felt reckless to me.

Yet her mystery was intoxicating to some. I felt a deep protective instinct, especially toward the youngest among us. I saw her approach a young woman who had confided in me about a previous traumatic experience with plant medicine. The young lady reminded me of my daughters as she was not much older. My chest tightened, fearing for her safety.

Healing cannot be rushed, sold, or coerced—it requires trust, presence, and safety. When we were alone, I cautioned her to decline the "ceremony." In that moment, I recognized a false teacher: someone offering the illusion of transformation while preying on the vulnerable. It was a sharp reminder that the tools we encounter—whether Kambo, yoga, or meditation—only serve the path when approached with respect, care, and discernment. True healing, the kind that makes us resonate at our highest frequency, always comes from within.

False teachers convey the idea that they themselves are the source of healing. And not all false teachers are humans wielding Kambo or mushrooms. Money can be a false teacher. A job title can be a false teacher. Alcohol can be a false teacher. A toxic relationship can be a false teacher. All promise to be the source of healing—and all can lead to new layers of harm, leading you away from the light.

It's important to remember that not all false teachers are malicious. I genuinely believe the British woman was trying to be helpful—but this is a dangerous risk to take with people who are actively exploring their own vulnerability on and off the mat. Just because someone has personally succeeded with a modality does not mean they are equipped to shepherd another's journey safely.

The true teachers are those who serve as a guide—who do not claim to be the source of healing itself but point you towards the source of healing already *within* you. They help you go inward to channel the energy within, to release the darkness holding you back. Otherwise, the "treatment," whether it be medication, natural remedies, therapy, or any other method, will not heal you—but will only exacerbate your condition.

MOTHER AYAHUASCA FOUND ME

They say Mother Ayahuasca finds you—you do not find her. And that was exactly my experience with this particular plant medicine. I had no exposure beforehand, and even to this day, I have not met another soul outside the group I was with who has taken it.

I wanted to learn about ayahuasca in a setting where sincerity and authenticity were alive, not as a curiosity or tourist experience. That's why I chose the Shipibo tribe of Peru. For them, ayahuasca is not just a brew— it is a living relationship, a sacred vine that teaches. The maestros who guide the ceremony are considered to have gifts from the medicine itself. It opens them to channel healing through song, through *Icaros*. These are not songs in the ordinary sense but vibrational tools, like a branch of mantra, carried on the breath and voice.

In the ceremony, the Icaros pierce the aura like a bee dropping pollen onto a flower, delivering exactly what is needed in that moment. Their sound is both medicine and guide, creating the environment in which healing can flourish—just as the ayahuasca vine flourishes by winding around the trees of the Amazonian jungle, drawing support yet offering its own resilience.

It was crucial for me to visit Machu Picchu and the Sacred Valley first, to understand this cultural and spiritual context before entering the retreat. I knew I needed to be grounded in the land and in the lineage, so that when I stepped into ceremony, I was not chasing an experience but entering a tradition with respect.

Taking plant medicine is not something you agree to simply because a stranger in a foreign land tells you to. Discernment is everything. These natural medicines can be profound tools for self-discovery, but they are not magic. They are guides, not sources of healing themselves. These ceremonies are to be treated with respect—not as recreation or experimentation.

I cannot say it enough: Ayahuasca is *not* for everyone. Nor can you trust anyone, because the false teachers are out there, waiting to rope you in.

You have to do your due diligence to make sure the people leading the ceremony are trained professionals. Do they have backup medical protocols? Do they have trauma training to help you process the emotions which will inevitably arise? When you neglect to test the intersection of teaching and healing, you put yourself—and others—at great danger.

In a 2017 article, journalist Barbara Fraser exposed this danger in her article "How Ayahuasca Tourism Jeopardizes Traditional Medicine."

"Some seek physical or psychological healing, and others wish for a spiritual awakening," she wrote. "Some say the experience gives them personal insight, helps to heal past traumas, or provides a way to deal with addiction."

One of the great dangers of the "Ayahuasca Tourism" trend we are seeing is that not everyone is going for a *healing* experience but purely for the *hallucinogenic* experience. And in some developing cultures—like Bali and in Guatemala—it becomes easier for false teachers to exploit the trend of wealthy Westerners arriving to satiate their curiosity.

With few—and often ineffective—regulations around plant medicine, it can be difficult for participants to know who a true, trained healer is—and who is there to exploit for their own gain.

Fraser observed the same:

"The industry's boom has come with a dark side. Some women have reported that they were sexually assaulted by shamans … There have been at least nine deaths at ayahuasca lodges in the past few years … although it is not clear whether any were directly linked to ingesting ayahuasca."

All of this on top of ethical and cultural concerns. In the case of recreational ayahuasca, it could be seen as a form of cultural appropriation. Especially when the participants are not being taught about the deeper cultural and spiritual aspects of the ceremony. The true purpose of the ceremony is in "waking up" to oneself, not in relation to others, though witnessing the awakening in others is critical to the experience.

Don't be deceived, though. You don't have to travel to a foreign country to find this dangerous trend. In America, we see a rising trend of ketamine treatments being used for depression despite the fact that the drug is only FDA-approved for use as an anesthetic. While it may be effective for some, we must always be wary of confusing a practice for the healing itself. They are *not* one in the same.

No method is ever one-size-fits-all. And putting your faith purely in the method is dangerous, no matter what it may be.

So while ayahuasca did wonders for me—it's not the path for everyone. As mentioned before, some people greatly benefit from talk therapy, though it did little for me. My fellow *ashram* colleagues found greater healing in breath work and yoga therapy. Likewise, your path to healing will look different—because you are different.

"Teaching is healing," they say. And I saw it—each of us learning from one another, each of us becoming teachers not by authority but by vulnerability. To teach was to show up as unfinished, as seeking, as willing to stumble forward.

In time, the greatest lesson crystallized at the ashram for me: you must become your own teacher. You must discern the modality, the rhythm, the portal that is right for you. For some, it is breath, for others mantra, for others still, movement or stillness. But the compass cannot be outsourced. The guru is within.

BECOMING YOUR OWN TEACHER

At the *ashram*, healing took many forms: the ballerinas learning to breathe, the addict steadied by music, the therapist humbled by vulnerability, and the subtle releases of others through laughter and tears. Healing is participatory, not performative. Teaching is healing. True teachers guide, but they do not claim to be the source. False teachers promise shortcuts, magic, or transformation.

By the end of my time in Rishikesh, the thread from that dark moment at thirteen—the pills, the despair, the whispered truth—wove itself into my practice:

You are not broken. You are becoming. Healing comes from within. The Healer is you.

True healing, the kind that makes us resonate at our highest frequency, always comes from inside. Methods, substances, teachers—they are tools. Your discernment, your awareness, your willingness to face your own inner darkness, is the source of transformation.

Before you can extend healing to anyone else, you must learn to process what is within you. You must forgive yourself for chasing false teachings, for harming others in ignorance, and for believing you were broken. Only then can you recognize authentic guidance, embrace the modalities that resonate with your spirit, and teach others by embodying your own growth.

During my month in Rishikesh, yoga taught me that I am my own teacher. It brought me back to the moment of my father standing over me when I woke up from my overdose attempt. It brought me through the darkness to a startling realization:

I had been holding onto the pain for many years—that dark energy my father had projected onto me. It had unleashed a monster within me that was tearing me apart, pulling me out of alignment. Without some help, I could not access the power within me to heal.

But once the awareness was there, it brought to me a series of revelations:

First—How carrying this pain caused me to act out of character, to inflict pain upon others along the way, perpetuating the cycle of pain.

Second—How I needed to forgive myself. We all must learn to first forgive ourselves, to release the shame we are carrying. Whatever your journey, you must learn to put down your own pain first. You cannot help anyone else until you have dealt with your own pain. You cannot heal others if you are stuck in the Victim Party.

Third—How I could not blame my father anymore. While I do not hope to have a restored relationship with him, that is not the point of removing the blame from him. As Irish-American author Malachy McCourt once quoted in an interview, "Resentment is like taking poison and waiting for the other person to die."

The point of forgiveness for me was to recognize that my father's behavior was the result of generational trauma. He too lacked true teachers in his own life—and therefore, he could never heal.

You might ask, "How could you forgive him?" Because I discovered that forgiving him is less about him and more about me making a choice to take back control over my story. Forgiveness allowed me to channel the Divine Feminine energy I so desperately needed.

See, when we discuss generational trauma, we often make comments like, "Mental health issues run in my family," or "Alcoholism is in my family." But in making these statements—both aloud and in our minds—we perpetuate the belief that we have no choice in the matter, that we are predestined to suffer. We are giving power to a narrative handed down to us rather than rewriting the narrative.

Instead, we must make the choice. The choice is an act of faith—to release the dark energy plaguing us and restore the power within. Only then can we begin to realign the light, to integrate mind, body, and spirit—to heal.

As I learned in my own ayahuasca experience, you have to digest what you ingest. What goes in must come out. That is, you must first process what is within you already—the positive *and* negative. Only then do you learn what to release. Only then can you find the right healing path for you.

You *will* be triggered—so you need a process—or ritual, if you will—to keep yourself safe. For me, I mentioned the process I call "Pray, Play, Create".

When I pray, it's about intentionally looking at what has transpired. Acknowledging the pain and hurt. It's having the *cois tine* fireside chat within, allowing the conversation to happen that can lead to integration. Finding where the shadow energy is—and then making any amends the next day. I take the time to forgive myself, to count my blessings so I can shift my mind to the positive.

When I play, it's through yoga, writing, or some other physical movement to release the negative energy I uncovered during praying. This too is *cois tine*—the dance, the song, the crocheting that transforms the internal into external. Through movement, I can externalize the negative, see it from outside of my own experience to reframe what happened. Play allows me to do a "software upgrade" within my own mind.

And with create, it's about applying what you have learned. It's about integrating mind, body, and spirit to self-actualize. And when you do so, it leads you to engage with others. This also is *cois tine*, the celebration of communal progress and healing.

It's natural to want to pass on what you learn—to give knowledge to others. It's the teacher within us all. But you must first ground yourself enough to manage what is within you. It keeps you humble in the knowledge that you yourself are not the source of healing for anyone else, though you can encourage them.

Beware the false shamans of the world. Even though they have the appearance of light, they will take advantage of your pain and lead you further into the darkness. Forgive yourself for the pain you've caused others and yourself. Forgive yourself for chasing false teaching. And forgive those who have wronged you.

When you do, you detoxify your spirit. You cleanse your mind and body. Then you can gain clarity on the teachers you need around you. You can embrace whichever healing method will channel the light within. And in time, you can teach others to find their modality for healing.

You do not need to travel oceans to find healing. It is here with you now. The Healer is within you. You are not broken. You are becoming. You are not alone. You are learning how to put your own pain down so that you can learn from and be present for others. In doing so, you begin to see that healing is not a solitary path; it is a conversation between your own inner teacher and the reflections offered by others, whose courage and vulnerability become mirrors and guides along the way.

CHAPTER 4
ABUNDANCE

In the literature of Ireland, I was introduced to two women who shared my name—one from legend and one from history.

One legendary Gráinne story mirrors that of King Arthur, Lady Guinevere, and Sir Lancelot. A beautiful princess, daughter of the High King Cormac Mac Airt is betrothed to Fionn Mac Cumhaill, the much older leader of the Fianna; a band of warriors that resembled a cross between King Arthurs knights and Robin Hoods outlaws. Gráinne in this case, elopes with the handsome warrior Diarmuid. It's a tale of tragic romance, scarcity, and pain.

The other historic Gráinne was of far more interest to my imagination—the queen of the high seas, Gráinne Ní Mháille—often referred to in British writings as Grace O'Malley. Taking up a life on the water as young as eleven, her father told her sailing was too dangerous because her hair might become entangled in the ropes.

So what did young Gráinne do? In an act of defiance, she took a blade and sliced off most of her hair, earning her the nickname of "Gráinne Mhaol"—that is, "Bald Grace."

With her father's death, she inherited the helm. According to folklore, her ship was attacked by rival Algerian pirates within an hour of giving birth to her son. So she strapped the young babe to her body and ascended to the deck to rally her crew to victory.

After the murder of her husband Donal O'Flaherty, it's said she recaptured Donal's castle, bringing vengeance upon her husband's murderers. And if you ever visit Ireland, you can still see her castle at Rockfleet in County Mayo.

In her later years, Gráinne Ní Mháille became a key figure in Irish politics, even being sent as an emissary to meet with Queen Elizabeth I at Greenwich Castle to broker a truce between her clan and the crown.

While it's difficult to separate fact from fiction, it may not matter. Gráinne Ní Mháille's life is full of energetic vibration. She was an inspirational balance of feminine and masculine energy. She secured independence for her people when much of the rest of the island was falling under British control. She was wholly herself in every facet of life—as rebellious daughter, as devoted wife, and as a fierce fighter, and as a fearless mother.

These parts of her being were not at war, they were unified within the warrior who is still known as "the Pirate Queen of Ireland." She is my namesake. My birthright. A bright symbol of abundance.

And yet, in emigrating to London, I may as well have forsaken this birthright. Though you could hardly find a more Irish name than mine, I no longer wanted any part of Ireland as my homeland. For me, my home represented only scarcity and pain. I exiled myself, and in doing so, exiled more of my spirit than I realized.

What I did not realize at the time was that across the map, another young woman called Tatiana, was wrestling with the same fracture of identity – hers draped in Russian syllables, mine steeped in Irish consonants. We would not meet until years later, but the symmetry of our stories would remind me that heritage has a way of threading lives together even when we try to sever it.

HERITAGE

In my earliest days of finance, I focused on ingratiating myself into Western corporate culture by learning the spoken and unspoken rules of the British workplace. One of my male colleagues had the bravery and boldness to speak the unspoken rules.

"Two things will hold you back here, Gráinne," he said in a flat, serious tone. "Being a woman and being Irish."

His words appeared unkind on the surface. And yet he made this declaration for my benefit—as a way to warn me of what I was walking into. He knew I was ambitious, that I longed to make a name for myself. And yet my very name was both Irish and female. Was my destiny already set by two parts of myself which I could not control?

Within my mind, I made a plan. If being Irish and being female would hold me back, then I would need to distance myself from both. I had just been given an opportunity to reach into the theatre days of my childhood to create a new mask for myself. Not for love of art, though, but to create a new identity, a character for myself.

Of course, I could not change my name or sex. But with this mask, I could alter the energy I exuded to the world. I stifled my feminine energies of nurture—and channeled the more masculine energies of ambition and dominance. In doing so, though, I did not realize how I was throwing off the balance in my own being.

Even more than the move to Donegal, I felt "othered" during my time in London. My Irishness weighed heavily upon me like a weight, drawing unwanted attention and derision. As far as I could tell, the Irish were at the bottom of the class system that existed in England. To make matters worse, this was a time when the IRA continued to make attacks, setting off bombs that would shut down the underground.

When the IRA bombed South Quay in 1996, it shut down the Tube. It was a long walk home that day. And when I arrived home to my flat, my British flatmate asked me, "Why are the Irish doing this?"

She did not say, "Why is the IRA doing this?" It was as if the detonator had been in my hand.

All I could say in return was, "I don't know."

I downplayed my Irish heritage to the point of allowing it to transform into shame. I drew a veil over my upbringing—and did so gladly, for I had finally escaped the scarcity of Ireland. I allowed myself to forget the good moments—the nights of *cois tine* and fireside chats, days filled with exploring nature alongside friends, the music of the ocean and the dance of the shamrock hillsides. All was pushed into the darkness.

The character I created for myself became more fully formed with each new role, each step up the corporate ladder. And then it met its peak when I moved to America and arrived on Wall Street. Not only in terms of my professional life either, but in my personal life, too.

In America, I met a man and married—which I viewed as the way to lock away my Irish upbringing. I was part of an *American* family now—one which could replace the brokenness I had seen in my Irish family. I settled into routines more than ever, sweeping away any hint of Irish ritual. Including the routine of a glass of wine every night to numb the gnawing voice inside saying, "Tear off the mask. You are meant to be *more*."

And yet something wondrous happened as my children came into the world and grew. The purity of their energy cracked open the door I had locked. It loosened the mask I had been wearing. With my son and daughters, the beauty of Ireland came rushing back to me. An energy within burst forth—a desire to connect them to their Irish heritage.

A civil war of identity erupted within me. My two names were in opposition to one another—the Irish first name given to me by a man who I wanted to escape and the married name that symbolized a hope for salvation. The irony is not lost on me now.

After the divorce, I especially had to resolve the friction in reclaiming my Irish identity again. The reconciliation with my heritage started through my involvement with the Irish Art Center in Manhattan, including speaking at a celebration called "Show Your Love."

Piece by piece, a love for my birth culture was rekindled. I saw it as a source of abundance which I needed to channel within me.

During the course of planning this book, I returned to Ireland for the first time in many years—like the prodigal returned home. My Uncle Noel, who was my father's older brother, had fallen ill again and I set my heart on seeing him once more.

In many ways, Noel had been more like a father to me. His was a soul that radiated warmth, humor, and kindness. He had been unemployed most of my life, due to being on disability and a long series of illnesses, including colon cancer.

Noel was so clever in how he spoke—like an Irish reincarnation of Will Rogers. He spoke directly and was a keen observer of the human condition. Noel was a great storyteller, able to turn a mundane event into a fantastical, hilarious romp. And while he never had many possessions, he collected more fridge magnets than anyone I've ever known, perhaps a symbol of his magnetic personality.

It was he who introduced me to so much of American culture, especially watching *The Wizard of Oz* on repeat. And he felt like a wizard to me— magical in his own right. Magical because he was the only person in my young life with whom I felt completely safe. I knew without a doubt he saw me as precious.

When I went to see him, I sat on his couch beside an empty fireplace— covered with blankets—to enjoy one last *cois tine* together. He shared a final "Dorothy" moment with me—him as the wizard, pointing me the way home.

"Do you see? Do you see?" he asked. "There's the screen, Gráinne, there's the screen. Put what it is that you need to put up there. You have all you need *inside*."

Isn't this the same message of the wizard to Dorothy and her companions? *"You have all you need inside you already."*

With Noel's passing, I felt the weight of the mask I had created for myself. The light in him connected with the light in me—the light he could see in me though I did not see it in full myself. He was my family—and he was *good*. He was Irish—and he was *good*.

While the process had already begun, his passing affirmed to me the need to reclaim my heritage. To embrace the abundance of my birthright through ritual—not routine.

RITUAL VS. ROUTINE

When thinking about the sacred fireside moments of my upbringing—*cois tine*—it could be easy to view them as singular events. On the surface, they may even appear to be no more than your average dinner party with friends and family. Yet if you were to feel the energy of the moment, you would recognize them as something else—a ritual.

Every culture has its own set of such rituals. The practice of yoga goes back thousands of years, first mentioned in the sacred text of the *Rig Veda*. For Muslims, the ritual is kneeling on the carpet for prayer five times a day. In Peru, I learned about the sacred *despacho*. A spiritual practice of laying down what burdens you with each new moon.

But no matter the culture or specific practice, all rituals share a common thread—they are a method for passing on ancient wisdom. They exist as a conduit to pass on energy—both internally and externally. Through ritual, we transmute energy through experiential wisdom—allowing us to vibrate within ourselves first—and then vibrate with others by witnessing their energy.

Yet in the commercialization of practices like yoga, we forsake the ritual. We divorce the sacred *asana* energy, relegating it to mere "exercise." Without the energy, it is no longer a ritual—but routine. The type of yoga many experience has been stripped down to a mathematical pursuit. No discussion of *dharma*, no sanskrit, no integration of what is learned on the mat which can be integrated into our existence off of the mat.

The problem with routines is that they force us to compartmentalize ourselves, whereas the goal for ritual is to integrate. And when you are caught in the rat race, compartmentalization of one's energy seems to be the more efficient way to find the elusive "work-life balance" working women chase after. It is only when the fruitless chase leads to utter exhaustion and burnout when so many of us have discovered the truth—compartmentalization created *more* imbalance.

We have traded our true identities for routines and we no longer recognize ourselves when we look in the mirror. In such a state, even our names begin to feel like labels devoid of meaning—an address for paychecks and bills. But we do not know who we are anymore.

If you find yourself trapped in routine—caught in a cycle of scarcity—your life ruled by a clock and rote responsibilities, then you are not alone. Far from it.

In trading my birthright for the picture of success, I lost my true self. This can be true for any version of success you find yourself chasing—yearning to have the perfect salary, or the perfect mother, or to be the perfect wife, the perfect mother, or the perfect friend.

But perfection is a lie and a trap. And the only way to escape it is through embracing our imperfections.

Routine strives for perfection. Ritual strives for balance.

And it was in my own search for balance at the *ashram* in India where my path crossed with Tatiana, who was in the midst of reconciling her own birthright—her own search for abundance.

LAYERS

Though we are nearly two decades apart , it became apparent that Tatiana and I were kindred spirits. When we met at the *ashram* in India, she was already well along the way in her own healing journey. She had already done so much of the work back in Paris where she lived, reading all the books, examining herself, and reconciling her identity.

Tatiana is half-French, half-Russian, but spent most of her childhood and early adulthood in Moscow since her mother and stepfather are Russian. But since her biological father is French, she would spend summers in Paris.

She never questioned her identity much growing up—this was her normal.

But all that would change in adulthood.

In 2015, Russia invaded the Crimean Peninsula, setting off a conflict with Ukraine that would later escalate in 2022. Russia's reputation in the global political climate tanked—and continued to plummet the following year when the sports doping scandal hit headlines. The global narrative became one of seeing Russians as power-hungry—a people who would do anything to get what they wanted.

Tatiana's heritage had just become a liability, like my own had when I was the same age.

When she was obtaining her French passport at eighteen, she had an opportunity to change her Russian last name to a French equivalent, but this was before the political climate had changed. After the Crimean invasion, she said, "There was a moment when I thought, 'Hmm, maybe I should have changed it.'"

Around this time, Tatiana finished her bachelor's degree in Geography, and decided to move to Paris for her Master's. Though she had spent nearly every summer in the city, she suddenly realized she had no sense of belonging in France—and desperately *wanted* to integrate into the French environment.

"I felt like my first stage was to completely abandon and completely shut down that Russian part of me," she shared with me. "I felt I needed to one hundred percent put an effort into talking like French people—acting, dressing French."

Like me, she put on a mask. She put on a costume. She became a character of what she thought she needed to be in the world.

But also like me, she couldn't hide from her name. Despite having a French father, her surname was Russian. Her name screamed her Russian-ness.

She would feel nervous sending her CV—ashamed of the Russian name donning the top of the document—afraid she would be discounted for her heritage. She deeply felt that being "the Russian in the room" was problematic. She always wanted to add a disclaimer— "Oh yes, I was raised in Russia, but actually, for the last ten years, I've lived in France."

When people would ask if she was Russian, she was ready with a sarcastic joke. "I'm not *really* from there," she would say, playing up her time in France—or apologizing for her Russian-ness.

She felt the conflict within her as well—warring natures. Growing up in a Russian household and schools, she had been taught to be a deep thinker, to embrace existential thinking in how she perceived the world. And while this certainly had its advantages in developing her mind to tackle complex problems and to excel in rational thinking. But it had its downsides, too.

"I was reading Dostoyevsky in the ninth grade—I was too young for that!" she recalled. "I realized that [thinking about all of these big questions] made me more prone to depression."

Meanwhile, her time in France exposed her to children who were able to more freely express themselves and be playful, creative, and curious. She saw how her French peers saw the world in an entirely different light, leading her to feel even more distant as she sought to integrate.

"We're not used to showing our emotions in Russian culture," she explained. "Being angry, being overly happy, being sad—this is not accepted. So that means you have this Inner Child in you, not allowed to act on what you're feeling."

What Tatiana didn't realize was how her upbringing was altering the way she channeled energy. She was putting a cage around herself—layers of fear and bias regarding her identity.She felt torn, like a person with no country, unable to reconcile who she was.

NUMB

After university, Tatiana took an internship for an international organization working on climate change policy. Before long, her drive led her to be promoted to a higher position. She was finding her identity in her work.

"In the beginning, it was all exciting," she recalled with a wide smile. "I was feeling like, 'Oh my God, I'm such a grown-up. I have such a fancy salary, I'm working for a noble mission to make the world a better place. In practice, I was writing policy reports that probably no one reads."

Yet she was finding these didn't satisfy the emptiness she still felt. She filled her after-hours with online dating, using men to validate herself, drinking wine every day, smoking on the terrace. She convinced herself these were all part of her desire to integrate into the French environment.

"You sit on the terrace with a cigarette and a glass of wine," she said. "Being all 'Frenchy' wearing all black, being all mysterious."

By the age of twenty-six, she was flying business class around the world, feeling important—but now the work had become less challenging, less stimulating.

"I started thinking, 'Oh, wow …is this it?' I felt so important … but then, in parallel, there was something missing."

Tatiana began to feel numb. She settled into a routine. Day in. Day out. She didn't feel happy. Or sad. And though she continued to excel at work, she felt nothing but routine.

"It was as if nothing was happening in my life," she said. "I wake up in the morning, kind of in a hangover. Go to the office. Go to the gym. And I kind of do all those things as if I'm a robot."

When she told me this, I knew exactly what she meant. It felt the same as my experience during my time at a very large New York-based bank. I had worked hard to assimilate into the character they hired—but then I was on autopilot. Numb.

To combat the numbness, Tatiana tried to motivate herself to become perfect. She was already efficient, but she wanted to build a reputation to be the best. "I was always thinking I should do this faster and better—but already, I was doing great and everyone loved me."

Like so many of us, Tatiana came from a family of high achievers. She had never allowed herself to be "good enough." Even while this taught her to have a strong work ethic and to be disciplined, it also taught her to *never* see herself as good enough. For her, this was normal. This was the routine—to never be fulfilled.

UNSTUCK

The tipping point for her came on the heels of an especially painful breakup. Tatiana was lying in her bed, experiencing insomnia in the middle of the night, feeling stuck and lacking forward momentum. In the stillness, a revelation came to her:

"I need help. I cannot navigate my life on my own."

It was at this moment she first considered therapy. She did some research and decided it was worth trying. Even though she would talk with friends about how she was feeling, she did not share everything. "I was not able to break this wall, and I felt just absolutely stuck … I was depressed, but I didn't know what depression is."

When Tatiana started therapy, she didn't know how to even discuss her feelings. "And the thing is, I remembered, until I was twenty-six, because of my upbringing, I never cried. Which is absolutely not normal. That means there are a lot of emotions that are just repressed and stuck and dragging me down."

Her therapist gave her the space to begin navigating her story—not labeling anything for her but challenging her to learn *how* to express herself.

"When I started therapy, I did not believe that it's going to help. For me, it was more like, I'm just going to try it out and see what happens," she explained.

"And then, through therapy," she continued, "I remember the first moment when I cried was when my therapist asked me to say something kind about myself … and it felt so bizarre, and I wasn't able to do it … and I just started crying, and it was so weird, but it was also so liberating. That was the moment when I realized that maybe something is working."

Tatiana began to notice some patterns in her life—how she would hop from job to job. She would feel excited for the first few months, and then descend once again into a state of feeling stuck, even though she was still rising the ranks. Which would put her back into depression again.

"I was not motivated to wake up in the morning," she said. "I had another depression cycle coming in."

And yet she also began to value the depression moments. As her awareness of them grew, she saw them as a driving force—for change.

In sessions, her therapist was using Gestalt therapy, where Tatiana practiced how to connect with her own internal emotional state, to understand what was within her. She learned how to bring her emotions to the surface safely—and name them.

Until then, she had never truly learned how to express sadness, how to express happiness. Or fear. Or anger—which was one of the most difficult emotions for her to face. Because for so long, she had been stuck—and numbed herself through all her various routines and coping mechanisms.

"When you went to therapy," I asked her, "were you drinking heavily to cope with the depression—or had you not related those two?"

"Back then I didn't relate those things," she answered. "But I was definitely drinking a lot to cope with depression. And that put me into more depression … I was reinforcing the cycle. I didn't tell my therapist that I was drinking … I felt too embarrassed and felt like, 'It doesn't matter. It's just my thing.' I felt like drinking was making me feel less lonely, like I had this friend with whom I hung out in the evening … I didn't imagine dropping it."

She also began to see how her stepfather's abuse of alcohol had attached itself to her. As a child, she had adored her stepfather, unaware of how his alcoholism caused him to detach. She spent years blaming herself, assuming a narrative of "I must not be good enough."

Tatiana had always assumed her childhood was happy, but by finally facing her emotions, she saw how problematic it had been. She went through a season of blaming everyone around her—but then saw how this was also unhealthy.

"I need to take responsibility for my life, because I'm the only one who can change," she said.

She finally admitted her drinking to her therapist, but started by sugarcoating the issue, saying, "I drink a little bit."

Eventually, she opened up more to say, "Actually, I'm drinking half a bottle of wine." And then she finally felt safe enough to admit the full truth: "Sometimes one, sometimes two bottles a day."

We often think of breakthroughs as sudden events—instantaneous transformations. But more often than not, it is like when a vehicle is stuck in the mud. At first, the wheels are spinning, spinning. You cannot get out of it alone. So you find someone who can help you push. At first, the wheels continue to spin, tossing mud around to the point it looks like an even bigger mess, and you feel awful that you've pulled someone else into the mess you've made.

But eventually, you move an inch. And then another inch. And with enough pushes, you gain traction and forward momentum. Only by acknowledging you are stuck and need help, will you begin the process of moving forward towards wholeness.

WHOLENESS

Through therapy, Tatiana was learning to accept herself; her full self. The good. The bad. And to start thinking of her life more holistically.

This led to her discovery of yoga. Before, she had always taken a siloed view of her life: Therapy was for the mind, the gym was for the body.

As she practiced yoga, her perspective shifted on how she saw the pieces of her life. But in the integration of her mind and body through the ritual of yoga, she saw how compartmentalization had contributed to her feelings of being disjointed and dissatisfied.

"There were different things that started helping me to realize that I can get better—and that I want to get better, that I want to feel better," she said. "Feeling better implies thinking about my life holistically. Thinking about not just how often I do yoga, how often I go to a gym, what I eat, but rather [to see] my life as a system."

"When I went to India for the first time for my first yoga teacher training, I saw a lot of people who thought differently," she recalled.

She noticed how the others alongside her were not trying to control anything—rather, they were "going with the flow." They were thinking about deep concepts like purpose, which allowed her to find a positive outlet for her existential Russian mind.

Surrounded by others and hearing the stories of their individual journeys helped her realize there was no single path to wholeness—rather, it was an individual choice. A choice she had the power within her to make.

"It gave me this sense of freedom, and it also gave me the sense of responsibility over my life," she said. "If I want to be happier, if I want to improve my well-being, there's no one who's going to change that for me. Nothing is going to fall from the sky. *I* need to do something. *I* need to change."

When she returned to France, her perspective of herself shifted. With the revelation that wholeness was a choice she could make, her attitudes and self-perception changed. She realized she did not have to choose between being French or Russian. She could fully embrace the beautiful parts from each culture and reject the parts that did not lead her to wholeness.

For instance, she found that she did not need to quit alcohol or cigarettes "cold turkey." As she practiced more yoga, she organically discovered those habits were incompatible with her own wholeness. She gradually dropped them—and yet she can still go out with friends and "be French" without a glass of wine in her hand. She could "be Russian" without condoning Russian aggression.

Through all these processes, she discovered an alchemy of healing.

"You never realize how you were hurting yourself before—through food, through interactions," she recalled. "I just felt like I didn't want to hurt myself anymore. Somehow, I turned all those processes—through therapy [and yoga]—I feel like it all aligned with this journey of self-acceptance, self-care, and self-love."

Her whole life up to now had been one lived out of scarcity—half-Russian, half-French, never good enough in school or work, always looking for a place to belong. But now she has learned to separate her identity from place—*to belong to herself first, no matter her physical geography.*

She also discovered the difference between routine and ritual in her own life. Until she started therapy, her whole life had been centered around routines—but routines tend to follow a scarcity mindset—taking actions without purpose. As she replaced routines with rituals, she was able to shift to an abundance mindset—seeing opportunity for growth and wholeness.

Tatiana admitted to me she still feels she has a long way to go. She shared about how during one of her yoga trainings, the teacher looked at her position and said, "Look at your left side—it seems like you're using your masculine energy way more."

She was amazed how much of this energy imbalance was showing through her movements and how her body could be a window into her spirit.

Let's not make the mistake of thinking we must shut off all masculine energy within ourselves to channel our feminine energy. Both energies have negative and positive attributes. The key is to bring the channels into balance—to find the middle ground so we are not relying on the maladaptive coping mechanisms prone to each.

"The feminine side is also about intuition, listening to yourself. It's about feeling that intuition and putting it into creating, into something you can make," she explained. "Whereas for me, masculine energy is more about rationality, how I'm supposed to act, what I'm supposed to do."

We need both for wholeness. If we shut down all masculine energy, we are still living half-lives, not embracing the full spectrum available to us. Routines force up to compartmentalize, to act from scarcity and choose one over the other. Ritual allows us to integrate our identity and energy—to find balance in the abundance.

BIRTHRIGHT OF ABUNDANCE

Tatiana's journey taught me so much about my own and how much I wish I had learned it at her age. Like her, I had viewed my heritage as a source of shame—a genetic disease to hide away. While our career paths were different, we shared a modus operandi—the mask of masculine energy. We put aside our identity in exchange for titles and salaries. Neither of us saw how we were trading the potential for abundance for a platitude of scarcity.

And for both of us, it took the pain of emptiness, the insidious pull of alcohol, and a breakup to wake us up. We were clinging to a shroud of scarcity, trying to warm ourselves, when the blanket of our birthright had been cast aside.

See, no matter where you come from, no matter your heritage, we share a birthright. Our birthright is not rooted in where we are born, how we were raised, or the blood flowing in our veins. Our birthright is abundance.

The beauty of this lesson is that you don't have to travel overseas to learn it. You don't have to wait decades to embrace it. You can seize it now, wherever you are. Because it's not about where you are, but who you choose to be.

Like my namesake Gráinne Ní Mháille, you can be an energetic balance of both masculine and feminine energy—babe strapped to your chest as you hold your sword high. Scarcity will tell you this is a conflict. Abundance assures you this is courage.

For much of my life, I've behaved more like the legendary Gráinne— putting my sense of self-worth and identity in external forces. And like in her story, it only led me to pain.

Instead, I needed to be more like the historic Gráinne—who trusted her intuitions above external influences.

In my own journey of healing, I learned to absorb the abundance available to me from my Irish heritage, and the abundance available in other cultures.

I've also learned to lay down the chains that have fettered me to scarcity for so long.

We do not have to live in black-and-white thinking. The world is full of a range of abundant colors. We can use whichever brushstrokes benefit us, and leave the others behind.

I saw this truth in my Uncle Noel. Though he never attained a high status in the eyes of the world through a job title or income, he was abundant in his attitude and in how he saw his place in the world.

He exuded a balance of masculine and feminine energy, which is why I felt so safe with him in comparison to my father.

In removing the mask from my life, in dropping the character of Corporate Gráinne I had fashioned, I have discovered a more complete version of myself.

Whatever mask you have put on, whatever character you have created from a place of scarcity, you can drop it. Identify the routines in your life that are keeping you stuck in scarcity, depression, and addiction—and replace them with the rituals that will lead you to abundance. Perhaps like Tatiana, it will be talk therapy. Or yoga. Or it could be prayer, deep meditation, or attending a support group.

Abundance is our birthright. Unlike our heritage, it is a birthright we get to choose. It is not often an *easy* choice, though. In the quest for good vibes, the path to abundance first requires some sacrifice. You will lose yourself in the process. But you will also find yourself. And along the journey, you will find others—sisters, brothers, and teachers who will guide you towards the light of good vibrations.

CHAPTER 5
LOVE

If you're worried this chapter is about to delve into a romantic view of "love" and finding your soulmate, fear not. Because this discussion begins with a septic tank.

Given how rural Donegal was, many of the homes were not connected to any kind of city plumbing. Instead, we had a septic tank. If nothing else, the presence of the septic tank made me more aware of the physical world and how it operates.

Depending on the fortitude of your digestive system, you might not want to eat a snack for this part.

Without getting too technical, the septic tank's job is to collect wastewater from your home and then naturally break it down with bacteria. As it breaks down, the wastewater is returned to the natural environment. In our case, the wastewater was reintroduced through an algae pond.

If you live in the city, you might be accustomed to being able to put non-biodegradable items into the toilet, such as chemical sprays or feminine hygiene products. But if you have a septic system like much of the world does, you learn quickly that you cannot do so. The systems cannot break down this type of waste, and you end up disrupting the natural processes of the environment.

And even when you were careful to handle your non-biodegradable responsibly, you could still run into other problems. Too many bacteria can build up in the system without warning. After all, the world of the septic tank demands a rather delicate balance in the pH of the system.

There were mornings when I would wake up—and the strong smell of sulfur would hit my nose. We all knew exactly what that meant. If the problem was really bad, then sewage would go back up the pipes, spilling into the house or into the garden, which then contaminated the soil and anything growing in it.

My father would have to go out to see if he could unblock the system—but if he was traveling or the buildup was too unwieldy, then we would have to call a service provider to come out and fix the problem. They would have to treat the system to restore the balance.

Typically, a backup valve helps prevent the worst overflows. But if the backup valve failed, you could count on a morning filled with embarrassment, knocking on the neighbor's door to ask to use their toilet or shower.

When I learned more about the human digestive system, I discovered how similar it is to a septic tank. Our stomach contains natural bacteria and enzymes to break down the biodegradables we ingest. And if we ingest what we shouldn't? The system wants to send it back up.

A 2007 study from Duke showed evidence that the role of the appendix itself is to be a sort of backup valve—a way to "reboot" the digestive system in the event of a buildup of bacterial flora. Or as the study itself described the appendix, "as a 'safe house' for beneficial bacteria."

And when we consider the connectivity of all our systems, it becomes even clearer that there is a brain-gut connection, which is where the microbiome comes into play. For those unfamiliar, the microbiome refers to the collection of microorganisms, mostly bacteria, living within the human body—specifically those which also play pivotal roles in our wellbeing.

Beyond supporting the digestive system, evidence is growing of the microbiome's role in regulating the immune system and contributing directly to brain health. Therefore, it's no stretch to see how the microbiome can influence and support mental health. The microbiome shows we are influenced not only by cosmic forces, but also microscopic ones.

When the microbiome is disrupted or thrown out of balance, it impacts our entire system. For instance, most of us have experienced "hanger," the negative mood swing that can occur when you haven't taken in enough nutrition for the day. Renowned child psychologists Karyn Purvis (Ph.D.) and David Cross (Ph.D) note this connection in their book *The Connected Child*, recommending that one of the first behavioral interventions you should take in trauma-informed care is to offer a child a drink and snack.

In retrospect, it now makes so much sense why I spent my entire teenage life experiencing colon issues, including irritable bowel syndrome, which led to multiple colonoscopies. Throughout my twenties, I was constantly going to the hospital for digestive problems, experiencing bloating, constipation. Much of it had to do with what I was eating, my bouts of bulimia, and the digestive process, but no doubt, it was also a result of the buildup of anxiety and trauma from my home life.

Buddhism and other faith traditions have noticed the spiritual connection between the gut and the mind, too—seeing the stomach as the center of enlightenment. This has led to more modern expressions about "trusting your gut" when facing a difficult decision.

And I received a rather visceral lesson in this when I went through an ayahuasca ceremony. I cannot stress enough that this is not something to enter into lightly or without understanding the cultural significance and physical ramifications. As you saw in my ashram story, these types of plant-assisted ceremonies can go awry when not performed correctly or when you are not in the right state for them.

In my case, I was with trained practitioners I had researched, and who had the resources available to deal with any emotional or medical situations that could arise from the ceremony. And thank goodness, because on the third day of the ceremony, I found my body purging years of toxicity.

Now one of my oft-cited mantras is "You have to digest what you ingest." Because if you don't, it *will* get messy.

So what does this admittedly disgusting analogy have to do with love?

Well, if your system is filled with an excess of toxic material—shame, hate, depression, isolation—then it will overflow into your actions. When life presents you with a new conflict or trial, you'll have nothing in your tank to bring balance. You'll purge the toxic sludge onto your environment, contaminating everything and everyone around you.

But if your system is filled with good material—love, kindness, joy—then these forces will break down whatever negativity life throws your way. The system will work the way it should, recycling the waste to the natural world where it can be purified.

If you are experiencing a lack of love in your life, it may have very little to do with your external circumstances. Your circumstances may be the final straw that causes the system to back up and overflow, but the root problem started long before.

Instead, the lack of love you're experiencing may be because you have a tank overflowing with toxicity. And likely, the toxicity is a combination of factors—not eating what you should, unhealthy relationships, scarcity mindset, and unhealed traumas.

When service providers came out to tend to our septic tank, they would often have to purge the system. They would have to pump out the excess bacteria and problematic wastewater so the tank could be emptied and refilled with the right material.

There is a wrong way to purge your system. And then there is a right way to do so, in which you empty yourself with the intention of making space for the right ingredients. If you want to become a source of love, then you must first be filled with love.

The hardest part for many of us?

Learning to love ourselves.

COMPETITION VS. CONNECTION

It would be fair to say I was something of "the teacher's pet" when I was in school. My teacher would often call me to the front to not only provide the answer to the question, but also explain it to my peers. And because of my love for Irish folklore, I learned how to read Gaelic and would be called upon to read aloud.

At the time, it felt empowering. To see my love of learning acknowledged brought me a great sense of self-worth. Especially when at home, my mother called me out for being too "quick," that is, "too clever"—for a girl, at least.

In hindsight, I can see where even these words created a competitive spirit in me. I felt like I was always competing for my mother's attention, specifically, competing with whatever soap opera was on at the time. Being told off for my intelligence was often the only way I knew to get attention.

Yet I was also unaware of how aligning myself more with the teachers created distance with my peers. Unaware of how I was trading the preciousness of childhood for precociousness. I was always the perennial "old soul," which made it far easier to connect with my teachers than with my peers.

On the occasions when I realized this, the pendulum would swing. I would act out and play silly pranks on my teachers—to prove I was not "one of them," that I was not a part of the establishment, per se, but a rebel. How often do we all do this when we feel the friction of not belonging?

So often throughout my childhood, the constant refrain in my mind was, "What am I doing here? I should be somewhere else."

I was spurred on to be the best, the brightest, to set myself apart from my peers. During my career, this translated into a toxic form of competition— a need to 'survive' better than everyone else, rather than looking for a way to connect with my peers.

Don't misunderstand me—there is nothing inherently wrong with ambition. But are you allowing that ambition to manifest as a way to elevate yourself, or as a way to elevate others?

Marie Curie is the only woman to have been awarded the Nobel Prize twice—once in 1903 for Physics and again in 1911 for Chemistry—and the only person to win in two different sciences. But her work was not predicated on winning a prize as a result of competition. It was motivated out of a desire to help alleviate suffering in the world—love for her fellow human.

If you're a driven, "Type A" individual, it is not a sin. But it is also not an excuse for creating distance between you and others, to see yourself as better than others. Rather, you can be a driven, Type A person in service to those who lack ambition, perhaps because they do not have the same resources available to them that you do.

So many of us have this "Type A Syndrome," which compels us to be perfect, to always be performing, to always be a master of whatever is put in our way. We suffer from a sense of "I don't want you to see me, who I really am within. I want you to see the task I've completed, the outcome I've won." Because deep down, we don't trust ourselves, and we're afraid that if we show ourselves to the world, then we will no longer be found acceptable.

We remain fixated on moving our own agendas forward—and seeing others as obstacles to overcome. When we feel "othered," we move into self-protection mode by "othering" others, even when they are being none other than themselves.

For myself, I viewed everything as a task—a routine. In my healing journey, I've learned to see everything as an opportunity for connection—a ritual.

Meanwhile, our Inner Child is yearning for connection over competition. She is yearning for the natural reciprocity that comes from authentic relationships with other humans.

And it's not always clear how to cross the chasm we've created between where we are and where we want to be.

So how do we bridge the gap? How do we empty ourselves of toxicity and believe that we are, in fact, worthy of love?

WORTHY

When I first met Sherri, it was clear we were kindred spirits. Not only are we close in age, but we share so many career similarities as high-achieving women in corporate spaces. Her journey made me realize that I was not an "isolated case," but just how common it is for women like us to channel our energy in the wrong direction for decades—achieving the outward signs of success while feeling less and less like ourselves on the inside.

And instead of clearing out our toxic tanks to make room for love, we fill them with everything else imaginable to try to feel worthy—money, junk food, entertainment, alcohol, relationships, status. But one by one, all these forces fail us. None of them leads to a sense of worthiness. If anything, they make us feel more worthless than before.

To become the full embodiment of love, though, we have to elevate the vibration. We have to believe our worth is not earned—but inherent.

Sherri's father was born during the Great Depression into a very poor family, since his father was ill. Still, he managed to be the first in their family to go to college—but as the sole breadwinner, his work kept him out of the house much of the time.

She grew up in a small, tight-knit community—the sort of small town where everybody knows everybody. Where everyone grows up together.

"I was an 'oops' baby ... fourth kid of five kids in six years," Sherri told me. "All of my siblings were at school. I was at home alone. My mom was distracted, addicted to TV, food, cigarettes. Not paying attention to me."

One of Sherri's earliest memories was when she was four years old, trying to get her mother's attention—competing with the soap operas playing on TV—and losing. Something in her clicked on at that moment.

"I am on my own in the world. Nobody was looking after me," she said. "And in that moment, I created a persona of [ambition] … I saw there was something about my little self, saw the pain in the world, and I was like, 'I'm going to do something about fixing this.'"

Though she lacked the proper language for it at the time, she had the perception to see that it was her father who had the power in the family, because he was the one who worked and made money. Even if her mother had wanted to leave her father, it would've been impossible—she had no resources to be independent.

"My dad was non-existent," she said. "I was never 'daddy's little girl,' so that comes with a whole lot of [feeling] unworthy, unlovable, all this stuff. So I chased worthiness through external power. That's why the titles matter. That's why the paycheck mattered."

"From then on, I cut off all play," she recalled. "I didn't talk on the phone with my friends. I was at the top of my class in everything."

For a while, she wanted to be a dancer, but then the powerhouse executive she was forming inside said, "This is useless—the arts are useless. Go play sports. That's where the power is."

The one source of community she felt in her teens was through sports—soccer, basketball, and track. And she held the belief that so long as she worked really, really hard, she could win everything.

"I wanted to win everything. I wanted to be a Class A soccer player, top of the list in the state. I wanted to do everything," she recalled. "And then, when my friends started to get involved in drugs and things like that, I didn't want anything to do with it … I just sort of stayed out of it."

"I was pretty straitlaced," she said. "I got 'Most Studious,' which sums it up."

Everything Sherri chose to do throughout her teen years was all about building her resume so she could get into a fabulous college and establish a fabulous career. And even to this day, looking back at those years, she realizes how isolated she was.

"I think I had friends," she said wistfully, "but I never felt like I was part of a group … By that time, I was really striving for this level of perfectionism that just doesn't exist."

When her senior year arrived, soccer was her best sport, and her team was on track to become a championship team, either winning the state finals or making it to the finals in all the subsequent years. But they got a new coach—and no one else on the team liked him because he coached so differently from the previous coach.

"So I tried to talk to him," she recalled. "I said, 'You're not coaching these girls the right way.' And for some reason, the other girls on the team got very threatened by that … Long story short, I found out that the entire team had been talking behind my back the full season. That was probably one of the most devastating moments of my life—to know that girls who I had grown up with were stabbing me in the back."

She only discovered this when it came time for the team to vote for MVP—and she didn't win like she had expected herself to. She was floored.

"I can laugh about it now, big deal," she smiled. "But back then, I was so tied to thinking I was on the right path if I won this award … I talked to one of my friends and she said, 'Yeah, nobody wanted you to get that anyway.'"

Suddenly, Sherri felt more isolated than ever. The one source of community she thought was there for her—her team—was no longer there for her because they saw her as allied with the coach against them. And she felt shame and embarrassment that she hadn't even noticed this for an entire season.

"To hide the insecurity I had, I gave off this 'I'm too good for you guys' … I'm going on to bigger and better things,'" she shared.

Rather than see her teammates as "mean girls," she internalized their actions. Sherri felt like, "I'm the mean one. I'm the villain of the story."

For someone who had made winning everything—including winning the favor of her peers—the revelation shook her very identity.

From that moment forward, Sherri's biggest trigger became the fear of being misunderstood. "It drives me crazy because I never thought people really understood me, and I don't think they did—nor should they. I probably came off like the most confident, the most driven ... I didn't dare give off the insecurity side—it was shameful to me. Like I was a problem. So it was a part of me that I hid because I didn't think people would respect me."

As much of a go-getter as Sherri was, the truth of the matter was she was getting her sense of worth from others—something she would only discover years later during her healing journey. She has since discovered that when your sense of worth comes from others, you give them all the power. You stop listening to yourself—your own intuition—seeking validation in the faces of everyone else around you.

VALIDATION

After being so dedicated and studious throughout high school, the betrayal of her lifelong friends and teammates taught Sherri one lesson—"If I'm to be worthy, I need a new personality." She did a 180 and became a wild child.

"I was pretty much drunk for four years," she admitted. "I had a lot of fun, and I definitely was not myself because I thought, 'nobody likes me.'"

But you can't keep a Type A personality down. Her Inner Go-Getter let Sherri have her personality break and then said, "Okay, time to get back to work now."

Her college had a strong program associated with a national insurance company—which provided her a route to end up in the corporate executive world.

"I got an economics degree, but I didn't know a lot about business," she said. "I was accepted at the Booth School for an MBA program. I thought, 'I'll go into sales for two years, make a little money, and then go back to get my MBA.' That was my plan."

But once she started working at the insurance company and weighed what she could make there against the cost of business school, she decided it wasn't worth it. She could make good money, move up the corporate ladder, and with their benefits, saw a future where she could have a family, work-life balance, and even travel.

So she stayed with the company for thirty years. She lived for her next performance review so she could scratch "the itch" of validation within herself. Yet review after review, raise after raise, promotion after promotion, the job never fully satisfied "the itch."

"I don't think it ever satisfied [me] … because I didn't achieve my goals," she said. "Because I was never meant to really be there. [Still], it served a purpose. I was able to get my kids through college and live a pretty decent life … but ultimately, I never really achieved my goals. I always came up against barriers."

Throughout those three decades, Sherri assumed the barriers were simply the obstacles she needed to overcome to reach the perfect title, the perfect salary—the perfect conditions which would finally validate her and make her feel worthy of love. It took her until recently to discover it was because she never loved insurance. It didn't spark any joy or love within her.

And how can you develop a sense of love for yourself when you don't love what you're doing? It's like trying to harvest tomatoes in a field where you only planted cabbage. And in the same way I channeled masculine energy as an adaptive method to "fit in" to the corporate mold, she found herself doing the same.

"I always thought I had to be almost a male," she recalled. "Shut your emotions down. Be an executive. That's the way to power in the world. Otherwise, you're just dependent. And I never wanted to be dependent on anybody."

When Sherri said this, it struck a chord with me. The whole reason I went into financial services was because of money—I had none growing up, and the industry had it all. I had equated money and power, so when my first position offered a signing bonus, it was a no-brainer for me. It felt like they were offering me power and validation.

But like Sherri, I always felt blocked. Even when I became infatuated with intellectual pursuits centered on the complexities of investment banking, I continually hit a wall. Something was always blocking me—and it wasn't about the money. It was about validation. And true validation can only come from finding your purpose.

"I did measure my success by the money," she admitted. "It's not something I'm super proud of—but it was a measuring stick for [answering], 'Am I doing okay?'"

Most of us—especially working women—seek external validation for our performance. Partly because of the expectations that we have to toe the line, especially when our acceptance by others, the validation we seek, is rooted in whether we are likable or not.

LIKABLE

In 2019, documentary filmmaker Robin Hauser delivered a TEDx Talk about "the likability dilemma for women leaders." In the talk, she talked about gender bias for women when it came to leadership positions—how likability often outweighed competence, especially in the workplace. Hauser's message resonated with Sherri, especially when she said:

"For as long as I can remember, I've had this insatiable desire to compete, to accomplish, and to prove myself. My energy isn't easily contained, and both men and women have called me intense, high-octane, aggressive …"

"The dilemma for women is that the qualities which we value in leadership, such as assertiveness and decisiveness, go against societal norms of what it is to be a likable woman."

Or, as Sherri summarized it for me, "Women have to lead straddling between being a bitch and a belle … And I always felt like that. I didn't want to be a total bitch. I wanted to be more vulnerable, a strong leader."

"Even in performance reviews, it was always, 'Sherri, you're too this, you're too that. You're too energetic. You're not energetic enough. You're too aggressive. You're not aggressive enough. Blah, blah, blah …' There was always this dichotomy."

This problem persists—not only in corporate workplaces, but also in politics and even in entrepreneurship, where the thirty-year average for female-led startups accounted for only 2.4 percent of all venture capital funding.

Perhaps you can begin to see the problem, if you have not experienced it for yourself. Women who have ambitions feel a need to shut down their feminine side because ambition is channeled through masculine energy. This is what many call the *double-bind*. If a woman leans into her ambition through masculine energy, she is seen as unlikable, but if she softens into her feminine, she is seen as lacking authority.

It's impossible.

What we truly need is a balance between the two energies. We need to create a space in which women can be ambitious and compassionate. Sherri said it beautifully in our conversation:

"We need more leaders who are vulnerable—leaders who lead with compassion that are more like Brené Brown," she said. "The women who make it to CEO, they start in finance—they don't start in marketing. They don't start in anything that's viewed as 'soft.' They are hardcore finance people. And I think there's an opportunity for both men and women to be more balanced in their masculine and feminine [energies]. They'll be better leaders. They'll have more follower-ship."

The catch-22 with likability is that no one can control whether another human likes them or not. It's too subjective. An expectation of perfect likability is prone to create discord.

So when our satisfaction, our validation, is contingent upon likability, it becomes all the more difficult to like ourselves. Like Sherri experienced, it becomes all too easy to say, "I am the problem." While this may be true some of the time, is it fair to assume *all* of the time?

Of course not.

Therefore, if we are to generate the good vibrations that will allow us to integrate mind, body, and spirit, to elevate, then we must first learn to like ourselves. And for many of us, the starting line for liking ourselves is not focusing on our strengths or our wins—but to dive headlong into our weaknesses and traumas.

NEGATIVE LOVE

When Sherri went off to college, she decided she was done with her family.

"I stayed on campus, and my parents would ask, 'Are you coming home for Thanksgiving?' And I would say, 'No, I have a paper to write.' And I would just stay by myself because it was just easier that way."

Sherri first tried therapy in college, but the therapist there didn't seem to know what to do with her. After all, she hadn't suffered from any "Capital T" traumas in her life, so she wasn't even sure what exactly to point to for the distress she was experiencing.

"I was in a shame spiral. And even the times that I was in such distress that I reached out to a therapist in college, I would leave there feeling worse," she recalled. "Their eyes would just get bigger, like I was abnormal. I had never experienced incest or abuse or rape or anything, but 'little t' trauma felt big for me."

Even with all the progress we have made with discussions around mental health, this is still a prevailing idea—that you only need help and healing if you have experienced one of the "Capital T" Traumas. Which feeds into the comparison trap—the idea that only certain pains are worth healing. That even in your distress, you are less deserving of help than those who have suffered worse.

But when you feel alone—when you are isolated and left to sit in your trauma, whether it's "big" or "little"—then this is when the anger seeps in through the cracks. And you try to push it down, but the more you push it down, the more control it takes over you. And so even a "little t" trauma can fester in the soul, like how a tiny germ can quickly grow into an infected wound.

By twenty-nine, Sherri was married and, in the years following, gave birth to her two children. On the surface, everything pointed to a successful life. But by her mid-thirties, she was divorced and still facing mental and physical challenges. This kind of duality in the inner and outer worlds of working women is not uncommon, despite how counterintuitive it seems. Her doctor recommended she look into a program called the Hoffman Process—an eight-day long personal growth retreat designed to help participants with identifying the destructive behaviors and mindsets that were unconsciously developed from childhood.

"The Hoffman Process is really about tackling the Negative Love syndrome," she explained. "As human beings, we are meant to be in tribes, so as a young person, your tribe is your family of origin … so you take on the characteristics of that family of origin. Which is why, in the pattern of abuse, the cycle just continues, because you take it on—even if you don't like it or reject it."

Hearing Sherri describe this took me back to my conversations at the Catholic retreat all those years ago—discussions of generational trauma. This is what the Hoffman Process would call "Negative Love," which is its own form of trauma. But for the first time, Sherri began to find some coping mechanisms that allowed her to discover and express her pain.

"I was pounding a pillow, getting my anger out," she described. "And then we did some visualizations—a lot of guided meditation."

One of these was an exercise in which Sherri mentally attended the funeral of her parents. All of a sudden, within one week's time, she went from being pissed at her parents to taking the leap to talk with them again.

And from there, she was able to move to forgiving them, writing them each a letter where she recognized the good they had done rather than only fixate on the ways she had been hurt by them.

Through these exercises, she alchemized Negative Love into Positive Love. She was able to extend that love not only to her parents but to her Inner Child as the first step in learning to love herself.

Learning to love herself opened her up to loving others—including Scott, her husband—a man who exhibits a wonderful balance of both Divine Feminine and Divine Masculine energy. By exposing the Negative Love, by facing it head-on, she was able to reconnect with her tribe and experience the alchemy of healing.

Yet, as I've said before, healing is a journey—not an event. And for Sherri to reach the next stage of healing—to become the full embodiment of love—she would have to go on a couple of journeys.

DIETA

For this last piece of Sherri's story, I must stress again that the healing journey looks different for each of us. We all have different starting lines in our lives. Different obstacles. Different pain. So in the same way that you cannot cure all physical maladies with a singular "miracle drug," not everyone should go off on an ayahuasca retreat.

Sherri certainly never saw herself doing it. Despite all the drinking she did in college, she had always been adamant that she wouldn't do any kind of drugs because she was convinced she would become an addict.

She first heard about ayahuasca from Scott, who had read about its psychedelic properties, its cultural significance, and how it was being used in healing ceremonies. "Do you want to go to Peru and do some?" he asked her

"Hell no," she replied. "No way, no how."

But as Sherri continued learning how to integrate her mind, body, and spirit, she found herself reading the work of Gabor Maté and about various healing modalities. She became more open to the idea of plant-based medicines and was interested in the concept of blending mental, physical, and spiritual healing.

During the last year of her time in corporate, she realized she was working nonstop and had no joy. She had lost all interest in her work. Still somewhat skeptical—but a curious skeptic—she started researching ayahuasca retreats.

"It's so important to go to a place that's reputable, that is focused not only on the medicine, but the integration afterwards—and also a place that's really trauma-informed," she said.

For Sherri, the concept of trying ayahuasca wasn't because she viewed it as a cure-all, but rather because she saw it as another possible healing modality on top of the work she had already done. Her gut told her it was time.

"Ten years ago, I wouldn't have been able to handle it. I think I would have had a psychotic break because I was not ready to face this part of myself," she admitted. "I didn't have the wherewithal to break that ego part of myself down until recently."

Once they found a place with great reviews and where they emphasized the integrative experience, they packed their bags and went off to Costa Rica in February of 2023.

Sherri was nervous going into the first ceremony—but found it to be a profound experience. She felt connected with the universe—and received visions of why she was worthy. She connected with her higher self, simultaneously finding a deeper connection to humanity—and purged a little as her system began to clear out.

"The big thing that I walked away from Costa Rica with is it's not all on me," she recalled. "I can trust some sort of higher power—whether you call that God, the universe, the soul, whatever—there are some forces outside of me that can let me relax a little, and it's going to be alright. I had never really been able to do that in my life before."

When she returned home, she felt a sense of rebirth—the birth of the person she was always meant to be. Without any hesitancy, she left her corporate job, though she had no clear idea of what would be next for her.

She and Scott decided to travel again, this time to Peru. Which was divine timing because it was there where we first met. During those ceremonies, she found more healing as she was now able to descend to deeper places of wounding under the compassionate care of our facilitator. During these experiences, she encountered a negative energy stuck within her body she dubbed "She-Devil."

Afterwards, Scott felt like he had experienced what he needed—but Sherri felt like she was still being called back to the Amazon. "Sherri, you hate the heat," he said. "You hate snakes. You're an indoor cat. What are you thinking?"

But she knew she needed to listen to her intuition and trust her gut. Instead of returning to the same ayahuasca retreat, though, she decided to go through the *dieta* experience. During a *dieta* retreat, individuals are isolated and given a strict diet of ritualistic foods as a way to purify the body, especially cleansing the gut flora.

Since her teenage years, Sherri had struggled with food. In high school, she would go days without eating and then overeat. And the toxic relationship with food became a cycle in her life, affecting her overall health and well-being.

"When you're a food addict too, you wreck your gut, which is the second brain," she said. "Which led to the depression. So I wanted to heal from all that."

She told Scott she needed to "wrestle She-Devil to the ground," and headed off to the Amazon.

"I lived in a hut for two weeks. I spent 99 percent of my time by myself, and my mind was racing the whole time," she explained. "We fasted for twenty-four to forty-eight hours with no water, no food, and then drank ayahuasca."

Now, remember my septic tank story from the opening of the chapter? How when it is out of balance an overflow can occur? And how sometimes, to fix the problem, the tank must be emptied?

That's essentially what Sherri experienced during the *dieta* ceremonies. She found herself being purged—physically, mentally, emotionally—and nothing she could do about it. This dieta was also a silent retreat, so even though there were others around, she didn't really know anyone else there or what to do.

"So there I was, sweaty and gross … just like a lump … I crawled to the bathroom, and [I'm] in a fast, so you can't even touch water. So I couldn't take a shower—but I'm cleaning myself up anyway," she explained. "I go back to my hut—it's two in the morning, and I'm just raging, writing in my journal about how humiliating [it was]."

Sherri was disgusted with herself and the experience—and yet it was also necessary. Her system needed to be emptied of the toxins that had built up over the years to create space for wellness—to create space for love. She realized so much of what she had purged was not only biological but spiritual.

"For the first time in my life, I'm not depressed," she said after the experience. "I have a sense of peace about me that I've never had … So even living in the unknown about the future—I'm scared about resources—but even with that, I have a sense of peace."

And I knew Sherri was telling me the truth because the woman I was speaking to at that moment—on the other side of the *dieta*—was different from the woman I had met in Peru. She was radiating warmth and joy, and peace. The darkness had been purged, and in its absence, her being was filled with light. She had become the full embodiment of love she was always meant to be.

LOVE AND BE LOVED

So many of us are seeking "good vibes" in all the wrong places. We become addicted to processed junk foods instead of turning to the abundance of nature. We become addicted to alcohol to numb the gnawing discomfort that we are meant for more. We compare our journey to others—minimizing our own pain instead of confronting it.

Let me offer this encouragement to you from Sherri's story—just because you haven't gone through "serious" abuse or injury doesn't mean you are less worthy of healing. Any of us can experience debilitating depression as a result of our genetic makeup, a breakup, losing a job, or because we are clinging to the regrets and mistakes of our past.

Sometimes the toughest love to achieve is self-love. Because no one knows you the way you know yourself. It will take time—years even—to learn how to love yourself. Perhaps it will come through the love of others. Or through processing your past, like Tatiana and Sherri.

How will you know the right path?

"It's always extremely important to listen to your gut," advised Sherri. "If something doesn't feel right, then it's not for you. And it doesn't mean it won't be right for you in the future, but it might not be right for you right now."

Trust your gut. It's speaking to you. It may need to be purified, but it will tell you what you need. What you ingest, you must digest.

And if you have been ingesting poison, then don't be surprised when it has to be purged from within. At the time, it will feel disgusting to confront the pain, the mistakes, and the humiliations. But in the end, you'll feel better for it because then you will have space for the love you deserve.

Healing is a journey—and the destination is to love and be loved.

Love is one of the highest vibrations of our being—it is the channel which can unite and balance both the Divine Feminine and Divine Masculine within us. As the great philosophers John Lennon and Paul McCartney wrote, "All you need is love."

And while learning to love yourself is key in the healing process, love is also generative. It does not terminate upon itself because it is an infinite source. When you are the full embodiment of love, you cannot help but want it to overflow into others. You cannot help but connect—to find your community.

CHAPTER 6

COMMUNITY

Over a century ago, French artist Jacques Majorelle bought a four-acre plot of land in Marrakech, Morocco. For the next four decades, the artist crafted two acres of the land into what may be his most enduring work of art—the Marjorelle Gardens.

What's interesting about the garden—besides its stunning beauty, of course—is why Majorelle came to Marrakech in the first place. Several years before purchasing the land, he had been sent to what was then known as French Morocco to convalesce from a serious heart problem.

He started his time in Casablanca before falling head over heels for the vibrancy of Marrakech, deciding to settle there and build a house. Where most would only see desert, Majorelle had seen a canvas. Unlike any other garden in the world, Majorelle cultivated over 130 species of plants from five continents—many of them cacti.

Perhaps the garden was the next step in his healing journey—but his original intentions appear to have been for his own pleasure. But due to the cost of creating the garden, he finally opened it to the public in 1947, charging admission to help offset the costs.

Today, the garden attracts around 700,000 visitors a year—including me in 2024. The land, which was once barren and lonely, now teems with community, drawn by a common purpose.

When I visited Marrakech, I was left breathless by the garden—an oasis of both life and serenity in the midst of the bustling desert city. And because it is a garden, Majorelle's work lives on—quite literally—still growing, thriving more than ever under the bright sun.

Cacti are typically thought of as a lonely plant, thorny and unfriendly. But in reality, cacti are survivors—proud and strong plants bringing color to otherwise void landscapes. They are a living contradiction—daring you not to touch them while inviting the eyes to embrace their unusual beauty.

They are terribly practical plants—storing water in creative ways, well-acquainted with the hardships of their surroundings. And they are even architectural in their design, with many cactus species stems adhering to the Fibonacci sequence, Mother Nature's original algorithm.

During my time in Marrakech, I was also struck by the call to prayers that would sound over the city five times a day. The hustle and bustle of the markets would cease as worshippers knelt on their carpets, faces turned east.

The ritual caused me to notice a wondrous contradiction within *salaah*—the Muslim act of prayer. It is both a solitary and communal act, simultaneously a spiritual and physical practice. And I could not help but notice the similarities to various yoga poses.

In both the Qiyam (standing position) of *salaah* and the Namaste of yoga, you see a physical example of balance in the positioning of the legs and feet. In both practices, you find a focus on mindfulness, concentration, discipline, breath work, and self-control.

Both practices are yet more expressions of *cois tine*, more evidence that our natural state is the integration of mind, body, and spirit, the channeling of the good vibrations from within us and from those around us.

If you feel like your life is a desert right now, then try to see it as a canvas of possibilities. You are a cactus—resilient, adaptive, and strong. We are all cacti within a garden—painting the earth with the thorns of our strength.

FLOW

I was first introduced to yoga while living in Hong Kong at the turn of the millennium. It was the height of the "cardio rage," and I was much more of a "gym rat." Looking back, I can see how my preferred workouts were a reflection of my go-go-go life: spinning, running, all cardio, all nonstop.

When I first heard of yoga, I was uninterested, to say the least. A practice designed to slow oneself down felt like utter nonsense. My thinking was, "The point of exercise is to get my heart rate up—I get more bang for the buck from cardio."

But when you live in a place like Hong Kong, it doesn't take long before you seek out community. I soon found myself plugging in with the British ex-pat community, and one of my fellow expats convinced me to try a class. A sense of cross-cultural curiosity finally compelled me to give it a try.

In many ways, my healing journey began there, though I didn't realize it at the time. Yoga brought out something from within me I didn't fully understand at the time. It showed me how to find the subtle body within me—to interact with my own life force and see that perhaps we are not human bodies with spirits, but rather, human spirits with bodies.

When I moved to Brooklyn, I joined a yoga studio run by one of my favorite teachers—Leslie. She was elegant yet disciplined, compassionate, and kind. She was the first to teach me the power of Dharma talk and the kirtan singing of Krishna Das —to hear truth and accept it not only in my mind but in my spirit.

From her, I learned the true nature of meditation. Before, I had the common misunderstanding of meditation as a solitary act of emptying your mind—an impossible task for someone like me. Leslie showed me how true meditation was about detaching from your personal experience so you can integrate with the collective. When combined with yoga, it allows you to transcend the automatic responses we've developed through routines. It disrupts the cycle like a "software upgrade" for the mind.

Some balk at the idea of self-care and self-healing as being self-serving. Yet what I've found to be true from my experience and the experiences of others is quite the opposite:

Self-healing is also collective healing.

When I left my job at Goldman Sachs, I worked with Leslie individually, so she would come over to my home to help me find my "flow energy." She was a spiritual teacher who happened to teach yoga.

But when Leslie left Brooklyn for California, I was on the lookout for a new teacher. Hot yoga was the current trend, but one I enjoyed because of how the heat aided my flexibility. Yet I held onto the lessons she taught me, constructing a narrative of who I am, where I come from, and where I'm going.

So much untapped wisdom is stored in our bodies—but we can access it by using the body as a vessel for this innate intelligence. Through movement, we can transmute the energy of our inner potential to connect with the potential of those around us.

Your DNA is more than derivative genetic coding. It is the evidence of life before you. You came to this moment now filled with the lives that preceded you. We are co-creations with one another. Our narratives are co-created. We may interpret our individual narratives through the lens of our experiences, but the nature of narrative is connection.

Which brings us to how I connected with Tamara, who became my new teacher in my crawl towards healing. Through her teaching, I would begin to understand the connection points between the individual journey and the collective journey of healing—and how it must come from a place of vision.

VISION

When she was only five years old, Tamara could visualize living in New York City. She had no dream job in mind—making a life for herself in the Big Apple was itself the dream. So it was fitting that her life followed a visual path, which led her to study visual arts in New York when she was twenty-four.

She had no real love for advertising, though she ended up in the field thanks to some early success with the likes of Revlon and Coty. I could sympathize with this part of her journey.

After all, my own path through finance and technology was utilitarian. I would have rather been an actress, a poet, or a teacher—but these were destitute paths.

Likewise, Tamara is an artist at heart—albeit the visionary sort. When she was promoted to being a creative director, it gave her the opportunity to sculpt the artistic visions of others.

"The best part of my job was in executing a vision," she shared with me. "I was really good at bringing a group of people together and letting them shine."

She thrived on gathering a community around a vision. So, if the firm was shooting a commercial, it was her job to hire the director, the makeup artist, the talent—all the essential people needed for the project. She would let others exert their talents, then step in to tweak it to create unity around the vision.

In this way, she had her first practice with combining community and vision, though she was doing it for corporate interests, not so much for the sake of humanity.

And so, she built a career working with top brands, hustling from one project to the next, losing herself in the noise. Like so many of us can attest to, the wakeup call came through a moment of searing pain.

In 2008, Tamara found herself abruptly laid off at the age of thirty-nine. The recession was at its worst, and suddenly, there was no place for her, and no jobs for anyone like her. "They kind of left me holding the bag," she recalled. "But regardless, it was a gift, because I ended up taking yoga teacher training."

Her decision to pursue yoga wasn't a vision like when she had dreamed of living in New York. But then again, her dream of living in New York had never been connected to a specific profession—so why not yoga?

"So it wasn't like I had a grand plan or anything," she shared. "It was just that I got laid off at the worst time that you could get laid off. There were no jobs.

And I said, 'I'm not going to sit around and wait for the phone to ring. I'm going to get out there and do something that I really want to do.'"

Not that she thought yoga would be the final answer. She had no idea what was involved in becoming a yoga teacher. But she heard about the training and knew she wanted to do it—not really thinking she would ever actually be a teacher. She did not find teaching—rather, it found her.

"When I started teaching and I walked through the fire of learning how to teach—which was very, very hard for me—I really loved it," she said. "At the training was where I feel like my life really changed."

At the training, the teacher asked them all to close their eyes and to visualize themselves in five years as if it had already happened. To her own surprise, Tamara found herself with a new vision:

"I said, 'In five years, I'm going to have a yoga studio, and it's going to be in Brooklyn,'" she recalled. "And then I put that aside and left it alone. I went back to my freelance career in advertising … because I had to make a living."

The funny thing about vision, though, is how it will lead you to take action, even when it doesn't seem to make sense.

"In 2013, I put together a business plan. I started looking at spaces. I didn't have any money, I didn't have a business partner, and I didn't have a dime to spend on this business," Tamara told me. "But I met somebody who was a real estate agent in the commercial wellness world, and she said, 'I'll help you find a space.' And so, I just went with it."

Nearly a year went by trying to find the right space for the studio in Brooklyn, and during that time, she also met with various investors.

"I'd never done this before. I didn't know what I was doing," she shrugged. "Most of the people in my life said, 'Maybe you'll do this in five years, that's a lot of money that you're asking for.'"

But Tamara just kept moving forward—all based on the vision that she would have her own yoga studio in five years. And not only did the real estate agent find her the right space, she helped her find an investor who ended up investing nearly three times what Tamara had initially been asking for.

"I couldn't have been handed a better business partner," she said, smiling. "A kind person and we aligned on pretty much everything."

In preparing the space, Tamara and her business partner approached it with a high design sensibility. Most yoga studios at the time were based around a blank, "white box" aesthetic. But Tamara wanted a space that was bursting with energy. She wanted the value for her students to go beyond the teaching itself. When they walked in the door, she wanted them to have an immediate sense of community, to be elevated by the space itself.

"It was like everything that I had led up to that moment, you know?" She smiled. "All of my career in advertising as a creative director literally set me up for this—because it was just a matter of bringing people together and letting them shine."

To a great extent, having a vision is a balancing act with control. On the one hand, control is an illusion. You can never know when you might lose a job, or a relationship, or anything. But you also can be intentional with the opportunities that come your way. Tamara could not control whether an investor would buy into her vision, but had she not been so intentional in her relationship with the real estate agent, then perhaps her vision would not have come to pass.

Likewise, when we can walk in an abundance mindset empowered by vision, our eyes can be opened to the opportunities around us. But if we are not careful, we can abuse the little control we do have, and soon find ourselves out of control.

CONTROL

Throughout my life, I've had what can only be described as a complex relationship with food. While never chronic, I've experienced bouts of bulimia. If I gained weight, I always had the sense this was a signal to the world proclaiming, "I'm out of control." The voices in my head would tell me, "You're shameful. Your lack of self-discipline is disgraceful."

My external circumstances didn't help. My mother would notice my lack of appetite—and seemed jealous over the control I exerted over what I chose to eat. She often seemed greedy and gluttonous in her relationship with food, so I had no desire to wallow in food myself.

And with puberty, the heightened awareness of the state of my body was only exacerbated. I was horrified by the stretch marks appearing on my hips—or perhaps horrified from a subconscious awareness of the danger in becoming a woman. Somewhere within me was a sense that my potential would be limited by my gender—that I would be deprived of the control I sought.

And so my coping mechanism was to control what I ate. I was aware of how others, like my mother, covered pain with food, and yet I was unaware of how I was doing the same thing, albeit through purging. I was judging her, not recognizing how hypocritical I was towards her.

Not to say this is wholly a female issue, it's not. But for at least the past century, men have faced less cultural criticism for their waist size than women.

And it should come as no surprise that eating disorders are not merely a matter of the body, but strongly linked to the wellness—or rather, un-wellness—of the mind. In a 2023 study, the Journal of Eating Disorders reported that "mental health problems such as depression, social anxiety, and ADHD were found to be more prevalent among people suffering from eating disorders."

Therefore, it stands to reason that those who suffer from an eating disorder as an attempt to control their environment will also suffer socially. The shame associated with food causes isolation and withdrawal from the community.

Tamara also found this to be true in her own struggles with food and control.

"I had a pretty intense eating disorder for about twenty-five years, from the ages of fifteen to almost forty," she admitted. "That really was the thing that held me back in life in so many different ways. When you have an eating disorder, it's really all about control, so everything was very limited for me."

"Everything involves food," she continued. "I wouldn't travel, I wouldn't have relationships … it was like being in a really, really intense hell … I literally was in a cage and could not get out. An eating disorder is very, very solitary and very shame-based. I was somebody who binged on food after starving myself for several days and over-exercising."

When she became more aware of the control food had over her life, Tamara sought out various methods of treatment.

"I did all the therapy, did all the things," she told me.

Tamara's therapist even recommended she try out Overeaters Anonymous, but she found it too depressing.

"[Alcoholics Anonymous] just looked like more fun, so I started going to AA instead—and I didn't have an alcohol problem then," she shared. "You know, alcoholism can be very glamorous in some ways. It's social."

So in a strange twist of fate, attending AA had the reverse effect on Tamara. Because alcohol was the more socially-acceptable vice, she later slipped into alcoholism as a new coping mechanism. Once again, she found herself in a contradictory state—trying to regain control by outsourcing control to a substance. Alcohol gave the illusion of control—while becoming a mask for the loneliness and disconnection she truly felt within.

The only treatment she felt like had given her any substantial relief was an antidepressant she was prescribed. It helped her conquer her eating disorder, yet by 2022, her gut was telling her she needed to leave it behind, too. So, after fifteen years on a high dosage of the same medication, she stopped.

"It was like taking the top off of a bottle you just shook up," she said. "I mean, I just exploded—the anxiety. I could not breathe … I'm really shocked I didn't have full-on panic attacks. And I [had] a lot of suicidal ideation—the window kept calling me."

Yet she trusted her gut. As she also stopped drinking, she ended up in the ER twice, panicking that she had done extreme damage to her liver.

"I didn't have anybody," she recalled. "I was so ashamed of what was happening to me, that I was all by myself."

And that's when she started meditating through writing.

One day, she was sitting in her living room and felt an energy within her compel her to pick up the pen and write. So she did.

All the agitation, all the anxiety, the spinning disc of her mind—she channeled it through her fingers and onto the paper, utilizing the writing method called The Artist's Way, because, at her core, she *is* an artist. At the time she shared this with me, she had gone nearly six hundred days straight of meditating. Though she started with writing, she soon added other meditation rituals—sitting in a sauna, taking freezing cold showers and plunges—and bit by bit, the practice of meditation brought her out of the hole.

One of her great revelations was realizing she had held the wrong idea about meditation for so long. The world of meditation can be very confusing and intimidating. Most people start with the premise that mediation means you cease thinking, which is impossible. At least, I know it is for me.

But Tamara found the real goal of meditation was not to achieve a blank state of mind, but to show up for herself—to empty the negative energy in whatever way made sense to her in the moment. Consistency mattered more than the methodology.

"It is not actually what I was practicing necessarily," she said, "but just showing up for myself. There's something in ritual and consistency and daily practice."

It's no stretch to say meditation saved Tamara. When she went off the medication, the barrage of suicidal ideation was constant. But by discovering what meditation looked like for her, she found a way to pass through the darkness—by allowing it to pass through her fingertips, alchemized into the ink of a pen upon paper.

Through meditation, Tamara continues to heal. She is learning to let go of the control she craved for so long, and by doing so, she is gaining something more important—balance in her energy. She is finding the good vibrations that so many are seeking through external sources.

Today, she is evolving her meditation, sometimes practicing in the morning, sometimes just before bed. When I spoke with her, she was in the midst of incorporating the Kundalini kriyas—chanting and singing along with writing. She uses it as a way to connect with her ancestors, asking for guidance and exercising gratitude.

So even with this mindset, Tamara is showing a side of meditation that few talk about. We often think of it as a solitary practice—but for Tamara, it is a communal practice. Even when she is alone, she is tapping into the ancient wisdom of her ancestors.

And this is nothing new for humans. Catholics invoke the saints in their prayers. Buddhists also seek the guidance of their ancestors. Muslims view prayer as communing with Allah—and they face Mecca as a way to recognize they are part of a larger community—as Muslims from all over the world turn to face the same direction.

If you find you are like Tamara and me, unable to hold the thoughts in your mind, then you should find hope in this communal view of meditation. Whether you are religious or not, you can see it as a practice to relinquish control—especially the forces controlling you—and to connect to a larger, universal wisdom. You can see it as a ritual of vibration—channeling out the negative energy around and within you in order to create space for the positive energy you need for daily healing.

Because healing is never a singular event—but a journey we are all on. We are eternally evolving alongside the universe, growing—and with growth comes pain. Perhaps the pain is the prompt we need to keep healing. And to do so together.

MALOCA

The indigenous people of the Amazon build long houses called *malocas*. And each community's *maloca* has distinctive characteristics representative of the community. Within a *maloca*, you'll find several families, usually with a patrilineal connection, living together.

These close living arrangements create an inherent sense of intimacy, which we might find uncomfortable in Western society. But in these indigenous societies, the *maloca* is an essential piece of how generational wisdom is passed down. As one source beautifully describes them:

"Your home symbolizes the tuning of the universe. The malocas reflect and are built through the memory and cosmology of the indigenous people that have been woven in their constant relationship with nature. This divine archetype personalizes the womb of Mother Earth, the house of the sun and the moon, or the receptacle of heavenly lightning. In it, knowledge is transmitted, contact is made with individual spirituality; on the other hand, it is also a political place where decisions are made for the community."

The indigenous people had the ancient wisdom to understand we are vibrational beings—we are constellations. We must connect to the universe, the earth, and the community to truly feel at home.

And this was how I felt when I entered Tamara's yoga studio the first time. She had opened in the midst of the gentrification of Brooklyn, and I had passed by the building many times, noting the line of people waiting to get in, hoping a space would be open for them.

When I finally went for myself, I was enchanted by the design aesthetic of the space—especially given how small it was inside. Because I am easily distracted, though, I always chose a spot at the front, further enhancing the feeling of being part of a tight-knit group in ritual together.

The danger we find ourselves in today—especially working women with all the demands upon us and the cacophony of social media—is that we can be surrounded by people and yet terribly isolated and lonely. And it becomes easy to believe you are in a community based on a number rather than based on the reality of your own experience.

What the indigenous people of the Amazon taught me is that *true community has little to do with how many people you know, but rather how connected you are to a group of people who know the true you.*

Even corporate America knows this with cliché adages like "quality over quantity," and yet in practice, most of us ignore this, seeking the latter.

Yet this is the essence of *cois tine*—a close-knit group of people gathered in a single home or in the local public house, sharing an intimate space, sharing the same breath, breathing in the smoke of the fire as the flames dance.

What Tamara loved about her advertising job had nothing to do with the ads—but about the community formed when talents collided. What she created with her yoga studio was similar—a community of people coming together into a meditative space where energy could integrate and connect.

You don't need to travel to the Amazon to find a *maloca*. Sacred spaces are not reserved for houses of worship but can be any space in which you can develop community. It could be your book club, a charity you volunteer for, a sports team—so long as you can be your authentic self with others. Like with meditation, there is no one method.

Earlier in the book, I shared how I felt more at home at my friends' houses than at my own house. Now I know the answer to why. Because "home" is not always the address where you sleep at night. It is not necessarily the walls you are obligated to pay a monthly rent or mortgage on. Home is where you feel safe and cared for—regardless of the geography. It is wherever you can be in tune with the universe while being yourself, safely.

Looking back at the previous stories, this same lesson of community emerges. For Tatiana, home could never be a specific country with her split heritage—but rather she had to learn to be at home within herself—and carry it with her. For Sherri, who had experienced pain from the people she saw as her community, she had to make peace with herself to find peace with others.

And so it was for me when I made peace with my Irish heritage. Home was not an island where I had faced so much shame. Nor any physical space, which is why I could never feel "at home" in any corporate environment I worked for, regardless of the job title or salary.

I have felt more at home swimming beside sharks in the Galapagos, doing yoga in an Indian *ashram*, or sharing a yoga session in my Brooklyn yoga studio. Because home is not a location—but within *you*. And you can access it freely when you are surrounded by an authentic community.

WARRIORS

In yoga, one of the hard opening poses often employed is the Warrior Pose. From a physical standpoint, the pose requires you to open your chest, your arms and your hip flexors. It is great for strengthening the lower body, core, and shoulders—as if you are preparing for a long journey where you will have to carry a burden.

Spiritually speaking, the Warrior Pose can be seen as a manifestation of opening your heart to the journey ahead. In the *Bhagavad Gita*, the warrior Arjuna is given spiritual guidance for the quest ahead of him as the god Krishna appears in human form.

In an English translation of chapter 2, verse 31, Krishna tells Arjuna, "Considering your duty as a warrior, you should not waver. Indeed, for a warrior, there is no better engagement than fighting for the upholding of righteousness."

We are warriors on a sacred quest—but we are not alone. In Joseph Campbell's storytelling framework, "The Hero's Journey," he describes the Helpers who come along to aid the hero in their adventure. Without the Helpers, the Hero may never step out their front door. In all such epic stories, there is usually a Guide who first initiates the quest, and then additional Helpers who come along at key moments to provide the Hero with whatever they need to endure in the moment of trial.

When I spoke with Tamara, she shared about the isolation she felt in her own journey—how separated she felt from others. So, I asked her how she even began to find community?

When you have no one around you, where do you get the strength to look?

Tamara said she expands the concept of community beyond the people who are near you.

"Because I felt so alone in my pain, I literally read every book, listened to every podcast, and watched every video from Elizabeth Gilbert, Cheryl Strayed, Dr. Joe Dispenza," she said.

"For example, Elizabeth Gilbert is probably one of my most intimate teachers, even though I've never met her or seen her in person. Because she's talked about this experience of being in an immense amount of pain and having suicidal ideation."

From there, she has expanded the circle of who she considers a guide on her journey to the stoics like Marcus Aurelius—one of my own favorites—and the aforementioned Joseph Campbell. By seeing herself as a warrior on a journey—in need of guidance—she was able to open her heart to the journey ahead.

But first, you must reorient your mind.

"Before everything else, you need to understand you are not your ego," Tamara said. A key moment in her journey was her own realization that her ego is a part of her mind but is not herself. She realized she was separate from it—that its job was to help protect her, but to also recognize that sometimes it wanted to protect her from dangers that were not real.

This highlights why every warrior needs a community of guides. Because the ego is always there, trying to protect you—but as Lord Krishna told Arjuna, the job of the warrior is to uphold righteousness. And oftentimes this requires the courage to venture onto the unknown path.

Doing so may come with criticism. And your ego wants to protect you from criticism.

Along the journey, you will face trials, setbacks, and opposition. But if you embrace your Inner Warrior, if you can open your heart to the journey, then you will see these as evidence that you are on the right path.

So, if you feel alone, like so many of us have, then first find your community through the resources at hand. Do your research to find your trusted guides, whether they be words on a page, a voice proclaiming truth through the earbuds you're wearing, your therapist, a spiritual leader, or the friend who you know loves you as your full self.

The biggest reason I sat down to have these conversations and record them here was to provide the sense of community I lacked for so long. Tamara and I both wish we had uncovered these ideas so much sooner and perhaps avoided some of the pain in our journeys.

And yet the pain is part of what makes us warriors. Persevering through it, learning to fight for ourselves and to fight for others. Your story is not yours alone. Your ancestors who came before are guiding you—showing you both the way to go and the ways to avoid. For only then can we grow beyond the ego to become the full embodiment of love.

CHAPTER 7
DESPACHO

Many have said, "You don't choose to do *ayahuasca*—rather, the medicine chooses you." That was certainly true for me. Before 2023, I knew nothing about plant medicine, nor had I met anyone who had experienced it. Despite going to raves in the '90s where psychedelics like acid and ecstasy were common, I'd never taken any myself.

Yet, just after I "fired myself" from corporate in 2023, something urged me toward this path. I sought a retreat grounded in indigenous healing practices, led by experienced facilitators who emphasized intention and integration.

You might recall that I had done extensive research before my own ayahuasca journey. So please don't read this story as a blanket endorsement. It is *not* for everyone. The beauty of learning how to integrate mind, body, and spirit is that there are so many paths to vibration.

But it would be inauthentic of me to leave out a more fulsome discussion of this piece of my own journey. Too often people enter ayahuasca with a tourist mentality. Or else, they believe it to be the source of healing itself. Let me assure you—it is not. But for me, it did play a role in my healing.

And so, I chose Peru's Sacred Valley to meet healers from the Shipibo tribe who are known for their deep connection to *ayahuasca*, which they also refer to as *la medicina* when speaking in Spanish.

Upon arriving in Lima, I quickly made my way to Cusco market, eager to explore the local crafts. Wandering through the streets early one morning, I stepped into an indoor market—a world bathed in color.

Bright blues, yellows, and greens surrounded me, reflecting Pachamama's (Mother Nature) bounty. Beautiful alpaca knitwear and tapestries seemed to carry ancient stories from the stars. It felt as if I had stumbled into a secret world, and my task was to explore and uncover its mysteries.

One stall in particular caught my attention. A young artist was hand painting t-shirts in neon colors that shifted in the light, reminiscent of work I'd seen back in New York from my Guatemalan friend. I asked if he could paint an image of the Uros women from Lake Titicaca, a place I would visit later on my journey. He agreed—and then suggested I talk to his father inside the shop while I waited.

His father, adorned with leather, feathers, and silver jewelry, had long dark hair pulled back, giving him the air of an owl—wise and all-seeing. His gaze, though piercing, wasn't intimidating. It felt like he already knew me, as though our encounter was destined.

As we exchanged words in a mixture of Spanish and English, he asked me, "Where are you from?"

"Irlande," I replied.

"Of the water," he responded. "And why did you come to Peru?"

"La medicina," I told him.

He nodded, understanding. "Show me your hands," he gestured.

I held my hands out, and he studied them, but without touching me. He then said, "You have tremendous power in your hands, but you cannot use it. Too many things on your back—like a *tortuga*, a turtle. You must put these things down." He continued, "Each moon cycle for eight moons, you must release these burdens, and then you can help others heal."

I was puzzled at first. My craft has always been one of the mind, not the hands. But I realized this was part of the reason I had come—to learn from those not conditioned by the same societal frameworks as I was, to embrace a reality beyond the physical.

The shaman—for that's what he was—reached into a drawer and produced an amulet—a necklace with a feather, a baby condor talon, serpentine, hematite, and turquoise stones, all set in silver with a number 8 carved in bronze. Never in my life had I seen anything like it.

When I offered to pay for it, he declined. "This is for protection and abundance," he said. "Place it just beneath the earth each full moon and release your burdens."

Respecting his gesture, I thanked him for the gift. But to honor the exchange, I paid his son double for the t-shirt. I cannot explain it, but wearing the amulet made me feel better prepared for the deeper journey ahead.

DIGESTING

Not long after, I arrived at the ayahuasca retreat in the Sacred Valley, a peaceful oasis at the foot of the mountains. A sense of pride filled me for my decision to come alone, trusting the process without needing a clear outcome. The other participants and I went through an orientation, in which we set our intentions for the first ceremony that would take place the next day.

Before describing my experience, it's essential to reiterate how this is not the only path. It might be easy for you to read this part of my story and think, "Well, I don't believe in such methods," or "I can't afford such methods," close the book, and settle for the ongoing cycle you find yourself in.

Keep in mind that this episode is a single chapter of my journey, not the whole story. Therefore, my recommendation for others is to always focus on the methods and rituals available to you in whatever medium is most practical. For instance, you may recall that Tamara redefined what meditation looked like for her—reading books written by teachers she trusted, writing in her journal every day, connecting with others in the community.

I believe this particular path of ayahuasca was set before me only because of how deeply I had buried my true self, because of how long I had worn the mask of the character of "Corporate Gráinne" I had settled for. Other practices like talk therapy had left me more wounded. The light within was so trapped, more extreme measures were needed to release the light.

And I can assure you—it was extreme.

Over the next few days, the plant medicine ceremony challenged me. I experienced intense abdominal discomfort and nearly left the retreat. Though I had been warned about the "purging" process (like what Sherri had also experienced), I hadn't anticipated how deeply it would affect me.

On the third night, the discomfort reached its peak, and as I made my way to the restroom, my body violently purged itself. This may be TMI for some, but it would be unauthentic to exclude from my narrative. Without too many grisly details, the experience felt like all my insides were pouring out.

In the midst of the purge, one of the facilitators came to check on me. I snapped at her, "The entire world just came out of [my ass]!"

Later on, I apologized to her for my outburst, but the intensity of the experience had shaken me to my core.

It was terrifying, and unless you've experienced it for yourself, it is almost impossible to describe. Yet it was also an undeniable release. I knew this was just the beginning of my journey to healing, of breaking down the old versions of myself that no longer served me.

Until that moment, I had been fighting to control the experience with my mind. I thought my mind could dominate my body. In doing so, I was actively preventing the integration of mind and body that I truly needed. So in that moment, I surrendered to the purge, despite the extreme discomfort and disgust I felt.

As I sat in the darkness, my inner dialogue spoke to me: "You have to digest what you ingest. There's no other way."

The truth resonated within me—the only way out of discomfort is not in bypassing it, but to pass through it. Afterward, I felt an overwhelming clarity. Everything in my life, every struggle, every trauma, every way I had been hurt and had hurt others . . . all of it had been part of my path. All of it could be released.

As the physical release happened, there were parallel mental and spiritual releases. It became clear that I had been holding onto illusions of control. What was needed now was to let go, to allow the natural flow of healing, to get out of my own way and put down the pain I had been holding onto for so long.

PUTTING PAIN DOWN

That night, I lay under the stars, much like I had years ago as a little girl in Ireland. My insides were quite literally emptied. Along with the emptiness, a stillness in my mind and spirit as I recovered. In this stillness, the shaman's words returned to me, like an echo vibrating from the stars above:

"You have to put your own pain down first."

I thought I understood, but I had only scratched the surface. Intellectually, I knew I needed to release what was holding me back, but I had no idea how deep that release needed to go.

The physical release I had just experienced was but the first step. It was a baptism of sorts—a cleansing of the old to make way for the new. You cannot clean the vessel filled with filth. You must first empty it. Only then can you scour the edges until they shine. Here I was, utterly scoured. Ready to be refilled.

For anyone who has experienced a menstrual cycle, there is a fascinating intersection of truth here. The womb must be purged before it can once again be restored to a condition where life can grow. And the biological female's body does this how often?

Every month.

The symbolism of the shaman's words were not lost on me. For life to exist, for growth to occur, we must be in a continual cycle of renewal. It's certainly not a pleasant experience. Menstruation comes with immense discomfort and pain, and yet it provides a picture for us to understand the same times of regular renewals we need if we are to vibrate to our highest levels.

The ancient Hebrews seemed to understand this. In their rabbinic law, women were considered "impure" for seven days following their menstrual cycle. Some have interpreted this use of impurity as sinful, but others have recognized that "being in a state of ritual impurity was not in itself sinful because menstruation . . . [is] part of normal physiology."

During these days of "impurity," women could recover from their pain. Their regular duties were lessened since anything they touched would also be considered "impure," allowing them to be restored. And at the end, they offered a ritualistic sacrifice to represent the realignment of their body and spirit, marking the release of pain and the symbolic restoration of fertility.

Going through menopause, women lose these physical reminders of these natural cycles of renewal. Ancient cultures connected the menstrual cycle to the idea of the Third Eye, that the natural circadian rhythms of the body provide supernatural insights. When the physical process is gone, we need new rituals to connect our bodies to the Third Eye.

The ayahuasca ceremony became for me a way to reconnect with these insights. It became a ritualistic sacrifice that gave me the space to be "impure" so that wholeness could be restored. However, on the other side of the ceremony, I needed an ongoing ritual. The need for purification is ongoing and it was unrealistic and unhealthy to rely on recurring ayahuasca use.

Clearly, the universe was ahead of me because the shaman had already given me a new ritual to follow—one which any of us can follow, regardless of our means. With each month, we can lay down our pain, empty the "impurity" within us, and be restored to new energetic fertility.

The ritual is known as *despacho*, "a means to dispatch or ship prayerful intentions off to the heavens." That is, a ritualistic method to intentionally release your pain to better vibrate with the energy within and around you.

NEW MOONS

The next new moon would arrive before I left Peru. Following the shaman's instructions, I buried the amulet outside where the moonlight could reach it. I meditated on what I needed to release. Over the coming months, I used this ritual to begin unraveling the deeper reasons why the energy felt misaligned in my life.

Through this process, I learned that every belief, every behavior, and every cycle I repeated was tied to an underlying truth that needed to be revealed, released, and restored. It was as if I were peeling back the layers of my soul, one moon cycle at a time. With each despacho, I gained clarity on what was "rotating" my soul—my beliefs, choices, behaviors, and self-awareness. Each cycle brought me closer to my true self, revealing the generative mechanisms behind my reality.

What I love about this practice is how accessible and flexible it is. Whether you are secular, religious, or curious, we all live under the light of the same moon. You can mold the practice to your own belief system because it's not concerned with a specific faith. Rather, it is concerned with the realigning of mind, body, and spirit by releasing the limiting beliefs you hold.

Releasing the eight beliefs my despacho revealed to me have transformed me. I chose to document them here both for my own purposes, to return to them as needed, but more importantly, because I have seen how common these beliefs are across humanity. Within these eight releases, consider which beliefs you also need to release.

Release 1: Love

My first release centered on my Love Belief that sounded like the following: "To love means to experience pain."

No wonder I believed this considering my upbringing. My picture of parental love was skewed through the lens of pain. The pain of the accident that left me scarred, the pain of every verbal and physical abuse from my father, the pain of feeling unprotected, unloved, and unseen.

These experiences created in me a false narrative of love—that love must inherently cause pain. And this belief tainted every relationship I had for decades. I was superimposing my false belief of love onto others, making me fearful of intimacy, of trust, and of being my full true self.

On some level, there appears to be truth in the belief. Which is part of why this can be so tricky to see as a false belief. Love often coincides with pain. Losing my beloved Uncle Noel was painful. Losing my marriage was painful. Arguments with my children are painful. Betrayal by a dear friend is painful.

You may recall that was the hangup Sherri had weighing her down for so long—the betrayal by her friends and the emotional distance of her parents also taught her that love meant pain.

Now, let's be clear: When you love, you *do* risk pain. However, this does not make love *synonymous* with pain.

Think of it like an automobile. When you enter an automobile, whether you're driving or not, there is always the risk of a collision. It can and will happen. Does that mean you experience a collision every time you enter a vehicle? Of course not. And so it is with love.

The strongest love may bring immense pain, but love also guides you out of the pain. To walk in love means putting down your own pain first. Only then can you be present to the truth in this moment.

Old Belief: To love means to experience pain.

New Belief: To love means to put down your pain first so you can be present to the truth.

Release 2: Fear

At the second new moon, I had to recognize that one of my supposed strengths was actually a gaping wound: "I fear no one. I've been hurt by those who love me, so what could be worse?"

For years, I had assumed that my tough exterior was a great strength, especially in corporate. No one and nothing could break through. But in the ritual of despacho, I realized that this was actually fear. I was so afraid of being hurt again that I had become a stony fortress.

Tatiana had a similar problem—her cultural upbringing had taught her that emotion was weakness. And she was so afraid of being perceived as weak that she couldn't open up. She had to continually maintain the exterior of "having it all together" even as she felt she was falling apart.

What we are really afraid of, though, is allowing our energy to lead us where we need to go. We are afraid of what the universe, God, and our own intuition is trying to teach us. We allow fear to throw a veil over the truth, giving power to the darkness when what we truly need is for light to pierce the darkness.

Old Belief: I fear no one. I've been hurt by those who love me, so what could be worse?

New Belief: I fear God when truth is concealed or not revealed at the right time. The enemy is always present—we choose when to engage.

Release 3: Scarcity

Growing up in scarcity, I thought the answer was to earn more money. And yet none of the money made the scarcity mindset dissolve. If anything, it only made it worse.

Within me, this belief said, "Scarcity is everywhere. One day, everything will be taken from me." My actions were constantly motivated from this sense of overwhelming scarcity, ready to take away everything I had gained. Instead, what I needed to learn was to stop, practice gratitude, and embrace abundance.

This was another lesson from Tatiana's story. She was chasing the appearances of abundance, all the while running from the emptiness she felt inside. The external could not fill the internal. She had to learn to start from the inside out.

We all have to recognize that scarcity is a self-perpetuating cancer of the soul. You can have every material possession you have ever dreamed of and still be stuck in scarcity, still afraid you will lose everything.

But abundance is our birthright. For all of us. It is a choice to be grateful, to be filled with the good around us, and allow it to overflow and pour into others. But we cannot pour into others if we remain empty.

Old Belief: Scarcity is everywhere. One day, everything will be taken from me.

New Belief: Abundance is a birthright. When there is space, we breathe into it. When there isn't any outside, we can create it within the body.

Release 4: Privilege

The next release for me came right out of the scarcity belief—recognizing my privilege. Though I came from poor means and faced biases throughout my life, I had to recognize I had reached a point of privilege. After all, here I was going to the Galapagos, Europe, India—those are privileges not available to everyone.

I had not realized that this had formed a toxic belief within me about how I viewed others. The narrative of privilege was, "My expectations are valid. People should follow rules and be orderly." Essentially, it was the mentality that "I have earned my privilege, so anyone can."

This isn't wholly true, though. We all come from different circumstances and are presented with different opportunities. Systemic forces can stand in the way of so many. Past trauma and family history cannot be discounted.

We saw this with Tamara's story. She had "followed the rules" of the corporate world, had reached the upper levels of her hierarchy and yet in a moment, it was taken from her. Privilege and position did not save her, despite "following the rules."

What saved her was her ability to harness a vision for the community. By stepping outside of the walls of privilege, she could release her pain of loss while embracing new potential in her yoga business.

We cannot place our own expectations on others. Rather, we should question our own expectations and whether they are truly beneficial for ourselves. Where privilege was once a toxic mindset, the release helped me reorient its purpose in my life. By releasing my old belief, I saw that I was no better than anyone else. I reframed privilege from a means to build myself up to being a way for me to build others up. I can use my position now to be an emissary, to help others negotiate their passage in life. I am no better than anyone else.

Old Belief: My expectations are valid—people should follow the rules and be orderly.

New Belief: There is no hierarchy in life. We are all free. Life is a negotiation of our passage.

Release 5: Self-Worth

In this part of the despacho process, I began to see how much of my self-worth had been tied to external validation—whether in my career, relationships, or social standing. I was so accustomed to working for recognition that I never realized I had built my sense of self on the shaky foundation of others' approval.

Also, I saw how interconnected the releases were. My faulty belief of love, fear, scarcity, and privilege were all feeding off one another. So, it was no surprise the next release I had to make was around my self-worth. My internal dialogue for my entire adult life had been, "I am only worthy if others recognize my value."

The danger of this belief should be obvious. We willingly outsource our worth to forces beyond our control, to the opinions and value systems of others—and then we wonder why we are so dissatisfied, so empty. This is the danger of being defined by a label or a single facet of life. If your sense of self-worth is connected to the shifting sands of money, relationships, politics, or job titles, then you will always be in a flux of dissatisfaction with yourself. You are forfeiting your value to other entities.

This realization was both liberating and humbling. I understood that I had been seeking worth in all the wrong places, projecting outward when I should have been looking within. Connection with the medicine unlocked the realization that my self-worth is not something to be given or taken away by others—it is part of our core essence. When we embrace this truth, the need for validation dissolves, allowing us to show up authentically.

Old Belief: I am only worthy if others recognize my value.

New Belief: My value is inherent. It does not need to be proven or performed. It simply is. I am valuable because I exist.

Release 6: Control

This belief was one of the most difficult for me to dismantle. As I reflected, I saw how often I tried to exert control over my life to prevent chaos and discomfort. In my professional life, in my relationships, and even in my personal healing journey, I had been subconsciously clinging to the idea that if I just managed everything perfectly, I could avoid pain or failure.

The medicine and the purging process were powerful teachers in this regard. When I finally let go of the need to control my body and allowed the medicine to work through me, I felt a profound release. I learned that true safety isn't found in trying to micromanage every detail but in trusting the natural flow of life, even when it is uncomfortable. The more I surrendered, the more I felt a sense of peace and alignment with the greater forces at play.

Control was another layer of narrative that drew me to Sherri's experience. So much of her life had been centered on what she could control—her grades, her performance on the field, her work performance. And the one time she surrendered control—her party days of college—had only reinforced the message that "I need to control situations and outcomes to feel safe."

But here is the hard truth we must all grapple with: all control is an illusion. And the only way to find peace within oneself is to surrender. If you're anything like me, this feels contrary. It grates against every atom of your being.

Yet ask yourself: Why are your emotions controlled by who wins an election? Why are you thrown into chaos when someone disappoints your expectations? Why do you feel the need to manipulate situations to get what you want? Because you are trying to wrest control from things you can never have control over.

When Sherri surrendered control, only then did she begin to find healing within herself—and within her relationships. Likewise, you'll find unexpected joy and safety when you surrender control and learn to trust the universe and be present in the moment.

Old Belief: I need to control situations and outcomes to feel safe.

New Belief: Control is an illusion. Safety comes from trust, surrender, and being present.

Release 7: Strength

Another tough belief to release because it meant overturning years of actions—and seeing the mistakes in those actions. I had long believed the narrative that "strength means never showing vulnerability," only to realize that vulnerability is true strength.

Growing up, I had internalized the message that being strong meant keeping it all together, never revealing weakness.

Vulnerability was seen as a flaw, a chink in the armor, something to be hidden away from the world. As a result, I built walls around my emotions, even when they were tearing me apart from the inside.

The medicine journey shattered the illusion that strength and vulnerability are opposites. As I sat in the rawness of my experience, particularly during the purging, I was stripped of any pretense. There was no choice but to feel everything and be present with my vulnerability. Through this, I discovered a new kind of strength—one that wasn't about holding it all together but about having the courage to fall apart, when necessary, to open up and allow healing to take place.

Here was another common thread between me and Tamara. No one who meets Tamara doubts her strength. But for years she numbed her vulnerability and pain through alcohol and other harmful practices. It was only when forced to let go and face those vulnerabilities that she untapped her true strength, first by putting her thoughts on the page, and then through connecting with others.

Being comfortable with your vulnerabilities creates confidence. Also, it builds rapport between you and others, thus strengthening the relationship. When you release vulnerability, you unleash your strength.

Old Belief: Strength means never showing vulnerability.

New Belief: True strength lies in vulnerability. It is in the courage to feel, to expose, to heal.

Release 8: Time

It's fitting that releasing my belief of time would be number eight because "8" is one of the symbols that represents infinity—the eternal. But instead of embracing the eternal within me, I lived under the pretense that "there isn't enough time—I'm running out of it."

This errant belief had been a persistent undercurrent in my life, pushing me to rush through experiences, to achieve quickly, to constantly strive without stopping to fully appreciate the journey.

I was always looking toward the next milestone, feeling that if I didn't reach it soon enough, I would somehow fall behind or fail.

However, the truth I found in despacho is that time is an abundant resource—if we choose to be present with it.

In the stillness of the ceremonies, I began to unravel my complex relationship with time. I realized that my perception of time had been warped by external pressures and internalized expectations. The truth is that time expands when we live fully in the moment.

As I connected more deeply with myself and the energy around me, I shifted to recognizing that there was more than enough time for everything that mattered. Time wasn't something to race against—it was something to embrace and flow with. Life is not measured by time, it's measured by *light*. With the time we have, we can make an impact on others that will ripple out through eternity.

Old Belief: There isn't enough time—I'm running out of it.

New Belief: Time is an abundant resource, if we are present with it.

INTEGRATION

Over the eight moon cycles that followed my journey, I took the time to sit with each of these revelations, meditating on how they were manifesting in my life. With each new moon, I buried the amulet just below the earth as instructed, and with each ceremony, I released a new layer of what was weighing me down.

The beauty of despacho, though, is that anyone can integrate the practice wherever and whoever they are. You don't have to go to Peru—you can do it from your back porch. You don't need an amulet. The amulet had no special powers—it only served as a tangible object to represent the release being made. Your amulet may be your journal, a coin, a ring, or anything else you choose. The ritual is what matters, not the object or geography.

In simplest terms, despacho is releasing negative energy to cleanse the spirit. And yet it also has the power to cleanse the mind and body when integrated.

126

The process of letting go was not always linear or easy. At times, I found myself clinging back to the old beliefs out of habit, comfort, or fear. But the despacho had given me a map, a way to navigate through the uncharted waters of my soul, and little by little, I began to feel lighter, more aligned, and more connected to my true essence.

I started to understand how the interconnected web of my beliefs, choices, behaviors, and ego had been shaping my reality. More importantly, the integration of new beliefs led me to see how much of my reality was based on false constructs—illusions I had built up over time to protect myself from pain or failure, but which were no longer serving me. And perhaps had never been serving me.

Through this journey, I learned that love, fear, scarcity, privilege, self-worth, control, strength, and time were all part of the same generative cycle. They are not separate, but interconnected, and by working through each one, I was able to return to the simple yet profound question that had guided my despacho: Does this belief increase love in the world?

If the answer was yes, then I knew the right path was before me.

This is the Heroine's Journey. What we are searching for in the quest lies inside. And yet we must go on the journey to find what has always been within. With the release, we can integrate. We can generate the *cois tine* within our souls, connecting us to who we truly are.

By releasing the old beliefs for the new, we integrate mind, body, and spirit. Only then do we connect the light within to vibrate at our full potential, to create the good vibes that bring true healing.

CHAPTER 8

VIBE

Stars are the original alchemists. They transform the elements within—hydrogen and helium—into pure energy. They create gravity, holding planets in orbit. Our sun reaches through our atmosphere where its energy is further alchemized into life—the grass, the tides, the sensation of warmth on our skin.

Like constellations, all is connected when the light crosses the darkness. Everything vibrates. Everything resonates.

When this idea is transferred into humans, the alchemy creates the Namaste Moment: "The light in me sees the light in you."

The labels we give one another fall away. The artificial divisions evaporate. When we vibe with our true essence, we vibe with one another. Our stories don't have to be exactly the same for vibing to happen.

I became very aware of the power of communal vibing after the murder of George Floyd in 2020. As a board member of the New York Women's Foundation at the time, I was becoming highly connected with groups across the city, seeing intersectionality at play.

When BLM marched the streets, I was proud to join them. My experience as an Irish immigrant greatly diverged from that of Black men and women in the United States, and yet pain is pain. From this point of darkness, I could see the light in my fellow humans. The light in me could connect with the light in them. I could also see that narratives were being woven that were not organic nor peaceful and that this story was far from over.

Vibrations exist on an inter-dimensional spectrum. Consider the vibrations caused from playing music. They vibrate us physically—impacting upon the tiny bones in our ears and sending electrical signals to the brain. Even those with hearing loss can feel the vibrations.

But these vibrations stimulate the mind as well. The right set of chords can call to mind words—lyrics we have not sung in years. From the storage files of our mind, music can access the data and bring that information to the forefront again.

And of course, musical vibrations can stimulate the soul. Certain notes or progressions can return us to memories of great joy or great despair. The sound of a weeping violin can move our spirits to great emotion—the body responding with tears.

Musical vibrations are the perfect analogy for what happens when we align the vibrations between mind, body, and spirit.

They are also the perfect analogy for what happens when those vibrations occur on the extreme ends of the spectrum. Too high of a pitch and the glass shatters. For years, sonic deterrants—sometimes known as "acoustic weapons"—have been used for dispersing riotous crowds, security systems, and even torture.

This is what I saw when the riots began. I had no idea when I marched with BLM that people would then start rioting and burning, wreaking destruction on the same communities they belonged to. The vibrations had moved too far away from harmony and into destruction.

As I watched a Target in Brooklyn set on fire, I was horrified by what I saw. It was a red line. I couldn't understand it. How could someone say they were protesting violence—with violence? It took me back to the Troubles of my childhood days in Ireland and the senseless acts of violence of the IRA against the British.

Such is the danger when we make a label ultimate. When we look to a label for healing or for belonging, then we outsource our vibrations to another spectrum entirely. Doing so can carry us too far into a destructive frequency.

The message here is not all "woo woo," fluffy rhetoric. Logic has its place. Decency has its place. Respect has its place.

These must be our boundaries so the vibes we channel do not overtake us and carry us into an unhealthy place. Vibing is not about being "woke," it is about being awake. Being awake to not only your truth, but the common truth.

When we fixate on labels, we are only staring into our own spotlight. We are fooled into believing we are enlightened because we "see the light," and yet we are blinded to everything else.

This is why we must see the light in others as well. Not only those who look like us, but everyone. We must stay within the realm of *namaste*, where the light brings us to peace—within ourselves and with others. While crossing the darkness, we must not cross *into* the darkness.

CROSSING THE DARKNESS

Good vibes don't come easy because there is a great conundrum with finding those good vibes—you must cross the darkness by facing the "bad" vibes.

Despacho forced me to find the bad vibes in my beliefs so I could rotate to new ones. The ritual showed me how these negative energies had metastasized and spread throughout my being—mind, body, and spirit. Now the real work began—the work that continues to this day. To find the cancer, excavate it, and allow the tissue to heal.

The metaphysical process of healing is not so different from the physical process. Crossing the darkness will scar you, yes—but the scars we bear tell our story.

In the Heroine's Journey, the alchemy of healing is a transformation of the 'wounded warrior' into the 'exalted being'. The lesson begins in the mind, in the vein of Descarte's pithy philosophy of "I think, therefore I am." However, if we do not act upon those thoughts, nothing happens in the material world.

This is the vibration—the force that moves us. We must control the apparatus of the mind first. The human mind is our greatest asset—and yet it can also destroy us. When we succumb to a false version of reality that is not our own. Delusion can devolve into psychosis.

The same risk faces us all when we dare to cross the darkness. Releasing the negative energy to cleanse the spirit must occur first—despacho. Otherwise, our own minds can turn against us.

You might wonder, "But why do we have to cross the darkness? Why not only embrace the light?"

This is where the typical sentiment of "good vibes only" falls apart. People make the statement with the best of intentions, yet fall short because they are not willing to cross the darkness.

Polarity is a natural function of the world—light and dark, positive charge and negative charge, yin and yang. If you think of the universe as a machine, both are needed for the pistons to work—the polarity creates movement. Without movement, everything dies.

Therefore, trying to cling only to the light is like the star that collapses into a black hole—it only consumes light. It no longer gives out its energy and its hunger is never satisfied.

Crossing the darkness is essential to vibing to our full potential. And if the polarity is off—if our focus is too much on the light or too much on the dark, then we must shut down the machine and recalibrate. Reset, renew, revive.

In every great story, the hero and heroine must cross the darkness. Persephone must descend into the underworld for spring to come. Christ must walk the Via Dolorosa before resurrection can occur. Lord Krishna must fight the demon before the path home is lit in one version of the Diwali tale.

And so it is with each of us. Cois tine is the lighting of the fire in the night. It is confronting the trauma, the false beliefs, and the toxic narratives which lock the light within.

You must put your own pain down first—despacho. Do not use your pain as an excuse to attack the world to extract vengeance. That is the path of darkness. Instead, we must cross the darkness with the light. We must embrace our unique journeys while celebrating the journeys of each other.

YOUR UNIQUE JOURNEY

Every woman profiled in this book had to cross the darkness—mentally, spiritually, and physically. This is the recurring theme for humanity, regardless of our ages, backgrounds, or core beliefs.

Your journey is your own. Do not allow your path to dictate the path of others.

So while Sherri and I both found great benefits with ayahuasca, neither of us would recommend it for everyone. Both of us had neglected our inner light for decades. Extreme measures were needed to cross the darkness.

Tatiana found healing through talk therapy. Tamara through writing and building a community.

Whatever your practice is that helps you heal, never treat it as the cure-all, nor judge others for the practices they need. We are on a common journey of healing, yes, but our individual paths look different, just as the constellations are all different from one another.

In the music of healing vibrations, we are each different notes. It is only when you have different notes that you can harmonize. And then there are those of us who change notes in the midst of the journey—our vibrations shift and alter as we heal.

During the process of writing this book, it forced me to cross the darkness again, to look at my pain with fresh eyes. I re-examine my own path in light of the paths others have taken, the identities I had taken on, and reassess whether those identities still made sense for me anymore.

For instance, I grew up in the Catholic religion, and while I liked the ritual going to church as a little girl, the religion itself left me feeling downtrodden.

In Ireland, Catholicism had been handed down as a function of national identity, another medium in which to express how we were victims of the Protestant British and now under control of the Roman Empire in the Vatican.

When I left Ireland, I left Catholicism. But not only Catholicism—I rejected God, the Bible, and faith altogether. I always remained a spiritual person, but my religion of choice became my own intellect and reason.

However, looking back, I now see that I need not have rejected God. He was not to blame for Irish Catholicism being warped into dogmatic ideology. I could instead choose to reject the victimhood. I could come back to the center of my spirit where belief truly mattered and catalyze faith as a force for good.

My rebellion was that I did not want to be one of the downtrodden. Financial security meant more to me than national identity, so I rejected anything that reminded me of home.

If the Catholic Church had weaponized the teaching, that was not my fault. It may not even have been their fault either but rather the rhetoric of the times forcing its way into the sacred spaces.

Likewise, I reexamined my political self. As an immigrant and a woman with a heart for underinvested communities, I aligned myself as a liberal in the US—and the far end of the spectrum at that—even as I was working in the beating heart of capitalism. Yet in light of the political polarization of recent times, the widening chasm between blue and red, I have found the reality of the world is that we live in the gray.

No longer could I identify with extreme ideology on either side. We need to become comfortable with living in the gray and to honor the wide spectrum of perspectives.

Politics doesn't allow for this thinking, though. Politics, by its very nature, is unforgivingly reductionistic and mathematical. It is a system of the masses in which you must choose sides and line up in formation. And yet this is not the only way.

We can and should continue to use the political process to drive change, to exercise our democratic rights. But when we "other" others for being none other than themselves, this is not "woke." We cannot hate on anyone for having a different reality than our own. Doing so is a waste of energy. It is the path of darkness, not crossing the darkness.

It is like the proverb that to not forgive is like taking poison and hoping the other person will die. In hindsight, this is exactly what was happening with me when I tried to kill myself with pills at thirteen. I didn't want to die. I wanted my father to die. But I took the poison.

For thirty years, my father was dead to me because he was the source of so much of my wounds. I had been abused, exploited—things had happened in front of me I should have never witnessed. No one was protecting me.

I piled all my blame on him. And while he may deserve this, did I receive any healing by doing so? Of course not.

Hate and vengeance *will* exact their toll from you. Perhaps not in such a dramatic fashion as a suicide attempt, but left unchecked, hate will grow like a cancer, and metastasize into shame, guilt, and violence.

The world is not always kind. Therefore, we must choose to be kind. To ourselves and to one another.

Therefore, if someone follows a different path than you in their healing journey, do not despise them for doing so. Their pain is not your pain. Their destination is not your destination. Our paths may cross at times—as mine did with these incredible women—but the vehicles we use to travel those paths will be unique to each of us.

Choose to see the light in others. They may not believe as you do, or vote as you do, or love as you do. But the same stardust runs in our veins. Choose to see the light.

Only then do we create cois tine with one another. Only then do we harmonize in the great symphony of life. Only then do we "vibe."

BECOMING THE WOUNDED WARRIOR

When the wounded warrior sets out on her journey, a sacrifice is required. Who you were must be left behind in exchange for who you will be.

The answers are inside of us, though we are continuously tempted to look outside. For years, I looked for healing in my job title, my salary, my relationships, and even by the anti-pattern of rejecting my Irish heritage.

This is why it was necessary for me to walk away from the corporate world entirely. I had to "fire myself," as it were. I could not authentically pursue the journey tethered to a broken system. I had to find the tools within.

In my first book, *Rotate*, I provided a set of tools that organizations and leaders can apply to be anchored in purpose and yet able to quickly respond to the needs of the moment while looking ahead to the future:

- Narrative
- Strategy
- Human-Centered Design
- Engineering
- Building Ecosystems

Regarding the wounded warrior in search of the energy that will heal her soul, I realized that a comparable version of these same tools apply to the healing journey, but they require new labels. Within each of us, we have five powerful tools we can wield as in the graphic below:

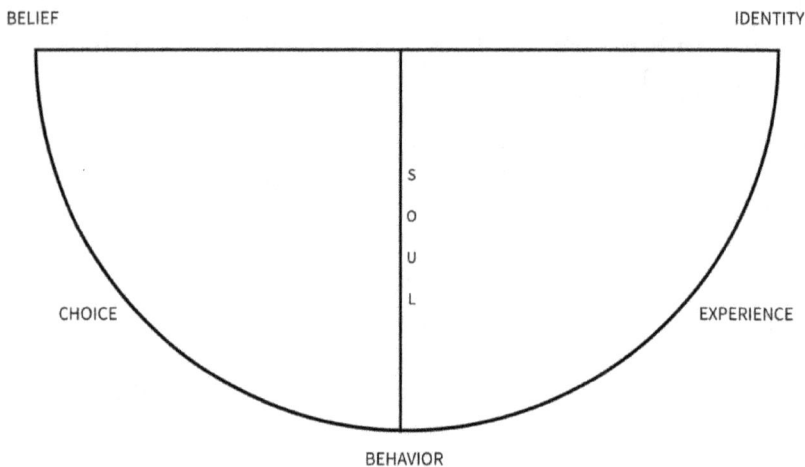

These are the tools you will need on your journey. And while all of these tools were present in each of the stories I've presented here, each story highlights one tool more than the others:

BELIEF

For my own story, the primary tool was Belief. Our beliefs about ourselves, others, and the world form the narrative we tell ourselves. When I look around the world today, narrative is being co-opted. It's being sold to us through headlines, through party platforms, through dogma. We are being told what to believe.

But narrative is a generative mechanism we own within our own mind, body, and soul. The discernment of truth comes from the soul. Our true narratives come when we align our beliefs with our mission and purpose and our own capacity for sense-making.

I had to let go of my old beliefs through despacho to make room for the new beliefs. By doing so, I shifted the narrative—from victim to victorious. From living behind a mask to dedicating my work to helping others feel safe to remove masks.

CHOICE

Our choices are rooted in the vision we see for ourselves. If we lack vision, we lack choices—in practice if not in reality. With vision, choices open up to us because we are no longer trying to control what is outside of our control.

Remember, Tamara always had a knack for vision, a key ingredient for her own healing journey. Being let go forced her to reevaluate what she truly wanted in her life. She had allowed her choices to be dictated by projects, by clients, by circumstances. Losing all that gave her the gift of autonomy, to align vision with purpose.

Mindfulness, meditation, writing, and reading allowed her to integrate her mind, body, and spirit so she could make new choices built on her new beliefs.

In this process, her choices built an ecosystem of healing through her yoga studio—developing a community of people who resonated with her energy.

Because her life is more integrated, she is more whole. Because she overflows with abundance, she is able to pour out into others, to guide them into integrating their own energies.

BEHAVIOR

Behavior is the link between our beliefs and our choices. With Tatiana's story, we saw the power of behavior when you make small changes to integrate your beliefs and choices. She struggled with her birth heritage—something she did not choose—and therefore assumed an identity that was not truly aligned with her nature.

Yet when she chose to make tiny changes in behavior—starting with therapy—those incremental changes had a compounding effect. As she chose healing over destructive behaviors, her world opened up. She was able to walk away from the hold alcohol had on her. She was able to choose her self-worth apart from jobs and relationships.

Previously her behaviors had been channeled through routines. Now her behaviors were channeled through rituals—aligning her identity to purpose. She could embrace her full self, breaking free from her people-pleasing behaviors to be fully empowered.

EXPERIENCE

As we saw in Sherri's case, she had no healthy feedback mechanism to gain perspective on what was happening in her life—that is, her experience of reality. Most people believe they are self-aware—yet you are never fully self-aware until you can recognize your impact on others. True self-awareness is others-awareness.

The betrayal Sherri felt from her teammates in school was symptomatic of this limited scope of self-awareness. And because she had lived on the assumption she was liked and admired by her teammates, it made the betrayal all the more painful. Throughout her life, she was so driven, so hellbent on her own designs, she was unable to receive the necessary feedback to understand how her actions were perceived.

When she went through her own ayahuasca ceremony, she reconnected with her inner child. She had grown so distant from her true self, she needed to engineer a bridge to cross the chasm between her true nature and who she had become. Her experience shifted.

By engineering the necessary channels to her traumas and building feedback loops of awareness, she is able to walk in gratitude and generosity, pouring into others.

IDENTITY

With my own story, we saw just how detrimental it can be to lose oneself completely, to lose all sense of your identity. When I could no longer center myself, it impacted my beliefs, my choices, my behaviors, and my experience. Everything was fractured.

When alcohol and job titles became a center for me, I quite literally lost myself, unable to differentiate my authentic identity from the characters I had created in the world to survive.

But when balance was restored to my spirit, my identity returned. Or rather, by centering myself, I found my true self again—I reconnected with my soul. I was able to separate from the ego, separate from the limiting beliefs and make healthier choices.

INTEGRATION

None of these tools can fully be put to use without the belt that binds them together, that integrates them. All these tools are essential, but integration is the key because it binds all the others together. It completes the loop so that energy can flow freely and allow the tools to work together in unison.

No one can practice these five tools perfectly, of course. The wounded warrior is not required to be perfect. We all fail and falter. We may resurrect old beliefs, make poor choices, or exhibit harmful behaviors. We may fail to be self-aware or fail to integrate our purpose and vision. What matters is that we continue the journey.

Literature provides a perfect example of what this looks like with the character of Frodo Baggins from The Lord of the Rings. In fact, you'll often find these particular books cited as one of the most effective large-scale literary examples of Joseph Campbell's Hero's Journey, reshaping it to argue that salvation comes not from heroic strength but from mercy and shared burden.

But for those unfamiliar, when the protagonist Frodo first sets out on his journey, he is whole. He is not yet the wounded warrior. It is upon the road where he is first afflicted with trials, hardship, and a wound that never heals. The journey is what makes him become a wounded warrior.

Pay attention. Let this be a key lesson. Your journey to healing may not have started when you were wounded. It may have started when you were still whole. Only in the processing of my own story did I realize this for myself. Forces were at play long before my birth that set the stage for my own healing journey.

Also, we should all find great hope in our mess, because while Frodo is the hero of the story, he is not always heroic. He can be indecisive at times—and sometimes makes the wrong call. In fact, at the penultimate moment of his mission, he chooses darkness over light. And yet he is honored for making it to the journey's end. When he returns home, he has a final chance to redeem himself and does so by freeing his beloved hometown. He only reached this point of redemption because of his previous errors.

Your wounds are not only obstacles—they can be opportunities. In Frodo's case, he ends his journey with three wounds we can learn from:

First, he is wounded by an enemy, by no fault of his own.

Second, he is wounded when he trusts the wrong person and is betrayed.

Third, he is wounded by the consequences of his own failure.

Does any of this sound familiar? We all carry similar wounds—the wounds that were no fault of our own, the wounds inflicted because we were betrayed, and the wounds we carry because of our own failures. The wounded warrior is not defined by the wounds, but rather by the healing.

One remaining lesson from Frodo. Throughout his journey, he has many tools available to him, some helpful, some not. Among the helpful tools are the sword that alerts him to danger and the mithril coat of mail that saves his life. Among the unhelpful tools is the evil ring that renders him invisible but corrupts his soul.

At times, it may feel like it would be easier to become invisible, to disappear, to simply slip into the shadows unnoticed. But doing so will corrupt your soul. It will eat away at you and eventually betray you to everything you fear.

Frodo's greatest assets are not the tools he carries—but rather his community. Every step of his journey is driven by his love for his people. And when he fails, his beloved friend Samwise is there to pick him up again. Sam never judges Frodo for his wrong choices. He is always a voice of encouragement and source of strength.

As wounded warriors, we all need a Samwise—and we need to be a Samwise to others. Because the greatest weapon of all is not our mind, our body, or even our spirit. The greatest weapon we possess is love.

INTO THE QUANTUM REALM

Much of what we experience in life—such as love, faith, hope—cannot be measured through scientific instruments. And yet we know they are real. We know they guide us in our healing journey. So where do they come from?

Throughout my healing journey, I became intensely interested in the idea of the quantum realm. As I became more attuned to how everything is connected within myself, I simultaneously looked at how all things are connected in our universe. So before we finish, let's pull out the metaphorical microscope and take a trip into the quantum realm.

It is no mystery there is a universal wisdom inherent to ancient cultures that we see playing out in our daily lives. You don't need to believe in God or any higher power to accept this idea.

Consider this:

Each atom of our universe operates as its own world. It has an electric charge—protons and electrons—positive and negative—balanced by neurons. The universe is simply buzzing with energy. And yet this energy is also what makes up all matter. Exactly what Einstein proposed by saying energy and matter are the same.

And yet this matter has always been in existence—yes, matter can be transformed into energy, but it cannot be created or destroyed. The building blocks are eternal.

Which is why it is so fitting for this final chapter to be the eighth—since "8" is a symbol of eternity, as mentioned in the last chapter.

The quantum connections are what allow knowledge to be encoded not only in your mind, but also in your body. The quantum realm empowers our intuitive intelligence—the eternal wisdom that has existed across time and space.

Your body—every atom within it—is made of an eternal substance, an eternal energy. You vibrate with the same energy as the stars. This is not mysticism or pure theory—but measurable in scientific terms. String theory is based on this concept—the idea in theoretical physics that reality is made up of infinitesimal *vibrating* strings, smaller than atoms.

When we are not vibrating with quantum forces, though, we feel the tension, the disruption. Because think about what happens when an atom is split—it explodes and wreaks devastation in its wake.

Perhaps that is how you feel now—like your atoms are splitting, like you are about to rupture. You are not alone.

The quantum realm is the great intersection of everything. Quantum is the place of equilibrium. When we integrate mind, body, and spirit, we are actually tapping into the energetic forces of the quantum realm, aligning back to the eternal cosmos. This is the "vibe" we feel. It is the vibe that allows us to connect with one another.

More and more, I come to believe that the quantum realm holds the answers to the greatest mysteries—why we experience love, pain, and hope. These ethereal forces come from deep within us, from the eternal.

It's why music connects the body to spirit. It's why intangible ideas can be transformed into tangible action. The vibrations begin and end within the quantum realm.

You might think of the quantum realm like "the Force" in Star Wars. It is the energy that penetrates everything and binds the universe together. We may know it as *the chakra energy center, or the life force of the prana, the* energy of enlightenment, the power of God.

Perhaps the quantum realm is even the source of reincarnation. Perhaps we ourselves are the reincarnation of stars, of the generations past who have already shed their energy, but the energy still carried their wisdom, their pain, and their hopes.

And one day, our time will pass, and the energy and matter of our atoms will pass through the quantum realm again—and return to the cosmos, recycled for eternity. We are not singular stars, we are constellations. Our stories are painted across the universe.

Look, I understand these are big, esoteric ideas. And yet the quantum realm can provide us with the greatest source of encouragement:

Your story is not over. Your story is only beginning.

In the quantum realm, many realities exist for you—many futures are open. The question is what will be your next move?

The power is available within you. The good vibes are within, ready to be channeled, to energetically integrate your mind, body, and spirit. You've already survived. Now it is time to vibe.

CONCLUSION

While this may be the end of the book, it is not the end of the work. If anything, it is the beginning. You must begin the work of unleashing the healer within yourself to integrate your mind, body, and spirit.

I hope you saw yourself in the stories here, that you were awakened to possibilities for how your journey can begin. Look at the Five Tools of the wounded warrior and use them.

- **Belief**—Identify the negative beliefs that you need to release. Then identify the positive ones that will unleash the love and light within you. As you form new beliefs, you will write a new narrative.

- **Choice**—Set a vision for your life and make decisions aligned with that vision. Choose to be in a community that will encourage you and support your vision.

- **Behavior**—Identify the small changes to integrate your beliefs and choices. Replace the routines with rituals.

- **Experience**—Create the necessary feedback loops to become more self-aware and others-aware. Reconnect with who you are in your essence to reshape your experience.

- **Identity**—Separate from ego and the character you've created from pain, limiting beliefs, and unhealthy choices. Reconnect with your soul.

The specific actions you take should integrate these tools. For example, my decision to give up alcohol:

Belief: "I'm dependent on this wine to release my stress" to "I don't want any substance to be my source of relief."

Choice: I chose to reduce my alcohol consumption and then eliminate it entirely. My physical health began to improve as a result.

Behavior: By eliminating alcohol from my life, I was better able to process my pain rather than numbing it. My mental health improved because I was no longer ingesting a depressant every day.

Experience: I became aware of how alcohol had numbed me to other aspects of my life and relationships. My self-awareness and others-awareness increased because I no longer had alcohol clouding my experience of the world.

Identity: Because I was no longer outsourcing pain to alcohol, I became more empowered in my spirit and self-assured in how I needed to show up for others.

Though it was not my intention, the integration of these five tools through my decision to give up alcohol has also brought me into community. Through my journey I met so many other women who had similar experiences with substances, whether alcohol or medications. We are able to encourage one another, especially given how socially acceptable drinking is.

The tools are not necessarily sequential, though they all stem from Belief, so I would encourage you to start there. Take a page from Tamara's book and begin writing your thoughts to gain clarity around your beliefs. There is great power in emptying your mind so you can better process your thoughts. You will be able to see which beliefs are beneficial and which ones are holding you captive.

If you feel lost, then celebrate. Losing yourself is where we all must start. You can now begin to find yourself. Along the journey, you will find others. You will reclaim the Divine Feminine and Divine Masculine by bringing balance to your energy, by elevating to the highest vibrations of your being.

Digest what you ingest.

Cross the darkness.

Release to unleash.

Separate from Ego.

See the light in others.

Though we are separated by time and space, the light in me sees the light in you. And it is beautiful.

www.ingramcontent.com/pod-product-compliance
Lightning Source LLC
Chambersburg PA
CBHW070906100426
42737CB00047B/2869